65-6600

AREOPAGITICA AND OF EDUCATION

English Classics — New Series

★

AREOPAGITICA
AND
OF EDUCATION

BY

JOHN MILTON

EDITED
WITH INTRODUCTIONS AND NOTES
BY

MICHAEL DAVIS, M.A.
*Senior English Master at
Marlborough College*

MACMILLAN
London · Melbourne · Toronto

ST MARTIN'S PRESS
New York
1967

MACMILLAN AND COMPANY LIMITED
Little Essex Street London WC 2
also Bombay Calcutta Madras Melbourne

THE MACMILLAN COMPANY OF CANADA LIMITED
70 Bond Street Toronto 2

ST MARTIN'S PRESS INC
175 Fifth Avenue New York NY 10010

PRINTED IN GREAT BRITAIN

List of Contents

▼

Acknowledgements

I wish to thank the following, who have kindly given permission for the use of copyright material: Messrs. Chatto & Windus, Ltd., for the extracts from *Milton and Wordsworth*, by H. J. C. Grierson, and *Milton*, by E. M. W. Tillyard; Messrs. J. M. Dent & Sons, Ltd., for the extract from *Milton Man and Thinker*, by Denis Saurat, and Messrs. Hutchinson & Co. (Publishers), Ltd., for the extracts from *Freedom of Expression, A Symposium*, edited by Hermon Ould.

I am also much indebted to the following editions and very grateful for the help that they have given me: *Areopagitica*, edited by John W. Hales, Oxford University Press, 1932; *Areopagitica*, edited by A. W. Verity, with a commentary by Sir R. C. Jebb, Pitt Press Series, Cambridge University Press, 1933; *Milton Prose Selections*, edited by Merritt Y. Hughes, Odyssey Series in English Literature, Odyssey Press, New York, 1947; and *Complete Prose Works of John Milton*, Yale University Press, Volume I 1953, Volume II 1959.

Many friends and colleagues have generously helped me with advice and criticism for which I am very grateful: I wish to thank especially Dr. P. N. Carter, Mr. A. F. Elliott, Dr. T. A. A. Hunter, Mr. D. A. Quadling and, most of all, Mr. E. G. H. Kempson. I also wish to thank N. J. Bardsley for his enthusiastic research on my behalf.

NOTE

I have modernized the spelling and punctuation of Milton's text and of my quotations from seventeenth-century writers.

M.D.

Introduction

THE LIFE OF JOHN MILTON

JOHN MILTON's father, the son of a well-to-do Roman Catholic yeoman from Oxfordshire, had been disinherited for turning Protestant. By profession he was a scrivener, whose work, combining that of attorney and law stationer, included the preparation of legal documents. He loved music, which he composed and performed very well, and his prosperous home in Bread Street, Cheapside, London, was a cultured one. Three of his children survived infancy: Anne, John — the poet — who was born there on 9 December 1608, and Christopher, the youngest by seven years.

'My father', wrote John Milton, 'destined me from a child to the pursuits of literature; and my appetite for knowledge was so voracious, that, from twelve years of age, I hardly ever left my studies, or went to bed before midnight. This primarily led to my loss of sight. My eyes were naturally weak, and I was subject to frequent headaches; which, however, could not chill the ardour of my curiosity, or retard the progress of my improvement.' Private tutors taught John Milton before he went to St. Paul's School, where, an able versifier in English and Latin, he stayed for four years until he was sixteen.

In 1625 Milton went up to Christ's College, Cambridge, intending to become a clergyman. He had auburn hair, a fair complexion and dark grey eyes: his gracious appearance and fastidious tastes earned him the nickname of 'The Lady'. He was an aloof and ardent classical scholar. Physically robust in all but sight, he took exercise by fencing. His conservative tutor found this eager, argumentative student rebellious, and Milton was sent down for a term.

After rustication, he returned to Christ's — although he was, as always, very critical of universities. He studied under a different tutor, and continued writing poems and prose in Latin and English. Disgust with Laud's tyranny over the Church of England prompted him to give up the idea of ordination, and when he came down from Cambridge in 1632 he withdrew to Horton, Buckinghamshire, where his father, nearing retirement, had recently gone to live. There, during nearly six years, Milton prepared himself by wide and deep study for a poet's exalted vocation. Greek, Latin and Italian literature, mathematics, cosmography and music were among his subjects. His writings at Horton included *L'Allegro*, *Il Penseroso*, and the Latin poem *Ad Patrem* which shows his affection for his father.

The old Countess of Derby lived near Horton, and for her Milton wrote the masque *Arcades* some time between 1630 and 1634. The music was probably composed by Henry Lawes, who may have suggested that Milton should be invited to write another masque, *Comus*, which was duly performed for the Countess's son-in-law at Ludlow Castle in 1634. Three years later, Edward King, Fellow of Christ's, was drowned on his way to Ireland, and Milton contributed *Lycidas* to a volume in memory of his fellow-student.

By 1638 Milton's mother had died, and his younger brother Christopher, a lawyer, had made Horton his married home. That April, Milton set off with letters of introduction and a servant on a foreign tour. He went through Paris to Italy, visited Genoa, Leghorn and Pisa and stayed for two months at Florence, where he talked with the literary leaders and academicians of renown, and visited Galileo. In Rome, too, he had other interesting discussions, and then moved on to Naples where, after a month, news of civil war in England reached him and called him back. 'I thought it base', he later wrote, 'that, while my fellow-countrymen were fighting at home for liberty, I should be travelling at my ease for intellectual culture.'

Perhaps Milton found that the first reports had been unduly alarming, for his return was leisurely. He spent two months in Rome, and then travelled to Florence. There, probably, news reached him that Charles Diodati, his close friend and schoolfellow, had died. The passionate Latin poem *Epitaphium Damonis*, written in memory of his idealized friend, makes clear the poet's deep personal grief. Before returning home, he visited Venice and Geneva (where he met Diodati's uncle, a great Protestant theologian), and reached England in August 1639.

Milton settled in London. His sister's husband had died, and her sons John and Edward Phillips lived in Milton's house in Aldersgate Street as boarding pupils. A few other boys, too, came to him for lessons. His work as a teacher did not prevent him from studying and writing, but his life was not entirely studious. Sometimes he would 'drop into the society of some young sparks of his acquaintance', and enjoy an evening of pleasure.

Already, he was meditating a major poem, but he still had not decided on its subject. The form was likely to be dramatic rather than epic, and four drafts remain of a tragedy in the Greek style on the subject of *Paradise Lost*.

Milton's poetic plans were indefinitely postponed, however, as he became increasingly absorbed in ecclesiastical and political affairs. Believing that religious liberty was incompatible with rule by the bishops, he joined in the pamphlet war on the side of the radical reformers who wished to destroy episcopacy. In 1641 he wrote his treatise *Of Reformation in England*, and followed it with four other pamphlets including *The Reason of Church Government*, which contains a long passage of autobiography. Poetry, he writes, is his real vocation, but duty calls him to serve his country with prose, although one day he will, in poetry, commemorate for ever the achievements of 'a great people'.

In 1642, Milton married Mary Powell of Forest Hill, near the Royalist centre, Oxford. She was sixteen, and came from a strongly Royalist family; he was more than twice her age, and the most formidable of the Puritan pamphleteers. The marriage was immediately a failure. After a month, the homesick girl, tired of her husband's uncongenial way of life, returned to her parents on a visit that Milton stipulated should last only a few weeks. She did not return for four years, and during her absence Milton's old father came to live with him.

Milton was deeply hurt and insulted by his wife's desertion. The law did not recognise incompatibility of character as grounds for divorce, and he considered that the law was wrong. He wrote a pamphlet, to be printed anonymously, on *The Doctrine and Discipline of Divorce*, in which he examined the nature of marriage and proclaimed that it was not sacramental. Only clerical superstition made it seem to be so.

Milton's unorthodox ideas shocked London. Undeterred, he brazenly issued an enlarged edition of his pamphlet, and dedicated it in his own name to Parliament and the Assembly of Divines. While public scandal about Milton and his revolutionary ideas was increasing, he published his treatise *Of Education*, and then addressed a further pamphlet on divorce to the clergy. The outcry reached a climax and Herbert Palmer, an eminent divine from the Westminster Assembly, preaching against 'ungodly toleration' to both Houses of Parliament, denounced the pamphlet as 'a wicked book abroad and uncensored, though deserving to be burnt, whose author hath been so impudent as to set his name to it'.

Milton turned from the subject of divorce (on which — although he had slight chance of altering the law — he was later to write two more tracts) in order to attack the censorship of printing. *Areopagitica* was published on 25 November 1644, but despite the eloquence of its noblest rhetoric this printed speech did not win freedom for the Press, during his lifetime.

Next summer the ill fortunes of the King's cause reduced the prosperity of the Powell family, who reconciled Milton and his wife. She returned with him to London, and they lived in the larger Barbican house that he had moved into because of the increase in the number of his pupils. Various members of the Powell family took refuge there after the fall of Oxford in 1646.

Milton's collected English and Latin poems, published at this time, caused little interest. For the next twenty years he was to be known chiefly as a pamphleteer. An account of his appearance and abilities has been left by his nephew, John Phillips:

> He was of moderate stature, and well proportioned, of a ruddy complexion, light brown hair, and handsome features, save that his eyes were none of the quickest. His deportment was sweet and affable; and his gait erect and manly, bespeaking courage and undauntedness (or a *nil conscire*), on which account he wore a sword while he had his sight, and was skilled in using it. He had an excellent ear, and could bear a part both in vocal and instrumental music.

In July 1646, Milton's first child, Anne, was born. The following January his father-in-law died, and two months later his own father, to whom he was devoted, died also. Milton felt desolate; and among his guests — the uncongenial Powells — 'I am compelled', he writes, 'to spend my life in perpetual loneliness'. However, the Powells soon went, and Milton and his family moved to a smaller house in High Holborn, with a reduced number of pupils. Milton wrote hardly any poetry there, but compiled three learned works and wrote a pamphlet, *Tenure of Kings*. This defence of regicide, which proclaimed his support for the Parliamentary cause, was published in February 1649 within a fortnight of Charles's execution, 'to reconcile the mind of the people to the event'.

A few weeks later Milton was invited, by the Council of State, to become Secretary of Foreign Tongues. He accepted the post, in which his chief duty was to translate outgoing dispatches into Latin and incoming dispatches into English. His annual salary was just under £300. He moved his home nearer his work, first to Charing Cross and then to apartments in Whitehall itself.

The Commonwealth regarded Milton as its chief literary adviser, and gave him a variety of tasks. One of the most important was the writing of a reply to *Eikon Basilike* (which means *The Royal Image*), an immensely popular book purporting to have been written by the martyred king himself. Milton's reply, *Eikonoklastes* (*The Image-Breaker*), was not a great success; but in 1651 his *Defensio pro Populo Anglicano*, a reply in Latin to a defence of Charles by Salmasius (a very learned professor at Leyden), was widely acclaimed as a triumph. During that year, Milton supervised *Mercurius Politicus*, a government newspaper issued twice a week.

In March his only son was born, but died an infant, and at the end of the year Milton, who was in poor health, moved to a house at the edge of St. James's Park. For a number of years his sight had been growing dimmer. One eye was already useless and, strained by over-work, the other now failed entirely also: from the age of forty-three he was totally blind. Much routine work was taken from him and, later, Andrew Marvell (the poet and M.P. for Hull) became his assistant in the Latin Secretariat. Music solaced Milton in his blindness: he played well on the organ and the bass viol, and he sang.

His wife bore him a third daughter and then died in May 1652. Milton mourned, and the household of the blind widower and three small daughters was forlorn. As Latin Secretary he worked harder than ever and, in the year of his bereavement, dictated a prodigious number of letters. Throughout the Protectorate he continued at his post. One of his notable works was the *Defensio Secunda*, published in May 1654; it contains elaborate praise of Cromwell.

Milton, whose health had improved, was courageous and cheerful in his blindness. He wrote some sonnets, and in November 1656 he married again. His wife, Katherine Woodcock brought him a brief spell of happiness before she died in childbirth fifteen months later. The child did not survive.

Milton and Marvell carried on their work when Cromwell died in 1658. Milton had probably begun *Paradise Lost* by that year. He continued to write prose and, until the eve of the Restoration, he issued pamphlets protesting against the Stuarts and prophesying disaster if Charles returned to England.

It is amazing that Milton's life was spared in 1660 when the King came to London. Dismissed from office, Milton took refuge in Bartholomew Close. The Commons voted that he should be arrested and his *Eikonoklastes* and *Defensio pro Populo Anglicano* should be burnt. He was arrested, but, probably by the influence of Sir William Davenant (Shakespeare's reputed godson and formerly poet laureate), whose liberty Milton had secured in 1651, and by the intercessions of Marvell and of other friends, he was released.

Milton was bitterly disillusioned by the Restoration. He moved to Holborn and then to Jewin Street, near Aldersgate. There he was neglected by everybody except his nephews and a few nonconformist friends. He depended on his three daughters and they, ill-educated and ignored in their childhood, spurned him. The eldest was not strong. Milton married his third wife, Elizabeth Minshull, aged twenty-four and thirty years his junior, in February 1663. They lived at a house in Artillery Walk, Bunhill Fields, and she probably made his home more orderly. He continued work on *Paradise Lost*, composing early in the morning and dictating sections of ten, twenty or thirty lines to whoever was at hand to write them down: if nobody was readily available, Milton would complain that 'he wanted to be milked'. In the summer he seldom wrote poetry.

To avoid the Great Plague of London, Milton and his family moved temporarily to Chalfont St. Giles, Buckinghamshire, and then returned to their London home. *Paradise Lost*, delayed by plague and fire, was published in the autumn of 1667, and 1300 copies were sold in eighteen months. Dryden enthusiastically proclaimed its merits. Milton, who had previously achieved fame through his Latin prose works, was now admired as an epic poet. Eminent visitors flocked to meet him at his house, where he was writing *Paradise Regained* and his last poem, *Samson Agonistes*.

Milton's life was now very regular. He rose extremely early, and worked all morning in his room, with someone to read and write for him. After dinner he walked in his garden or, in wet weather, used an indoor swing for exercise. Part of the afternoon was given to the enjoyment of music. At about four o'clock he spent an hour alone, and after that he was accessible to friends. His conversation at meals was extremely pleasant, sharpened with satirical wit. He rarely drank between meals, and his use of wine was always temperate. About nine o'clock 'he smoked his pipe and drank a glass of water, and went to bed'. He suffered much from gout, but when the pain attacked him he would bear it patiently and even sing.

At this time in his life Milton attended no church. He devoted Sundays to the reading of the Bible and of commentaries on it, but despite his own profoundly devout nature he did not hold religious observances in his household, even for the benefit of his daughters. They left home in 1669 'to learn some curious and ingenious sorts of manufacture', embroidery in particular.

Paradise Regained and *Samson Agonistes* were published in 1671 in one volume, and two years later his last pamphlet, *Of True Religion*, and a second edition of his *Poems* came out. In 1674 the second edition of *Paradise Lost* appeared.

On 8 November 1674, when he was nearly sixty-six years old, Milton died at his home, with 'so little pain or emotion that the time of his expiring was not perceived by those in the room'. He was buried in the church of St. Giles, Cripplegate, beside his father.

AREOPAGITICA

Introduction

I. THE BACKGROUND

1. WAR, POLITICS AND RELIGION

Areopagitica, whatever its lasting value as literature, is firmly rooted in the place and time of its writing: London, 1644. Charles had made Oxford the Royalist capital of England, but London remained the Puritan centre of Church and State, exposed to intermittent threats of military attack and defended by trenches that her citizens had dug the previous year.

Political and religious arguments blazed in London during 1644. The heat of them still smoulders and glows in the heaps of pamphlets — many of them demanding freedom of thought and expression — which her presses poured out at that hectic time. Milton's pamphlet, *Areopagitica*, is directed at one instrument of civil repression, a particular Order of Parliament: but his general passion for religious and political liberty shines from its pages, and his ardour ranges widely.

At the time when he wrote *Areopagitica* the military situation gave hope to the Puritans. In July, Newcastle's army had been destroyed at Marston Moor in the battle which laid the whole of the north open to Parliamentary forces. Prince Rupert's cavalry had been defeated, and Cromwell's was now the most powerful in England. But the military situation also gave the Puritans uneasiness. During September, Charles had outmanoeuvred the Parliamentary forces in Cornwall: their leader, Essex, had been forced to escape by sea, leaving his infantry to surrender at Lostwithiel without fighting. Milton's alternating tones of bright confidence and dark misgiving reflect the military feelings of the time, although *Areopagitica* does not refer in detail to the war.

Many of Milton's allusions to civil and religious affairs are direct. More than three years had passed since Charles signed the Bill which forbade the dissolution of the existing Long Parliament without its own consent, and exactly three years

B

since the Puritans in the Commons won, by a small majority, the motion to abolish episcopacy. Now Archbishop Laud's hated regime was ended and his power broken. Milton recalls in *Areopagitica* how Laud had enforced ritual in parish churches by episcopal visitation, had prohibited evangelical practice and preaching in the Church, and persecuted nonconformity outside it. The indignation with which the Primate's rule was remembered can be heard in Milton's caustic comments.

However, in 1644 the possible results of another three-year-old Puritan success, the Grand Remonstrance, caused Milton profound misgivings. The Grand Remonstrance had demanded and won a Parliamentary reformation of the Church, to be drawn up in accordance with Presbyterian principles but subordinating ecclesiastical to secular power. Convocation had, inevitably, been abolished with its leaders, the bishops. But now Milton wondered whether its successor, the Assembly of Divines, (then meeting at Westminster to mould belief and worship into a form that Parliament would impose), was going to prove just as restricting. Were the hopes for a Church to be made up of free congregations, governing themselves, doomed to failure? Was 'New Presbyter' indeed going to be 'but Old Priest writ large'? He was deeply apprehensive about the answers to these questions, which were more topical than such ills as Star Chamber, monopolies, ship-money, tunnage and poundage. All those old sores had been remedied in accordance with Parliament's demand, but their pain lingered and Milton deliberately aggravated it in his discussion of two intimately related subjects close to his heart, freedom of expression and religious liberty. These are the two main subjects of *Areopagitica*.

2. CONTROL OF THE PRESS: LICENSING ORDERS

The Licensing Order which prompted *Areopagitica* was passed by Parliament on 14 June 1643, but the Press was officially restricted in England centuries earlier. In 1408, even before the introduction of printing, the licensing of books was instituted. Although at various periods the regulations were generally ignored, the policy was reiterated and used many times, often by Protestant reformers. Among the monarchs who proclaimed it were Henry VIII, Elizabeth and James I.

In 1637, Charles I established, by Star Chamber Decree, a control of the Press more elaborate than any before or since in England. All undesirable books and pamphlets were banned, licensed books had to be relicensed before being reprinted, and no works could be printed without the author's and printer's name. The printing trade was regulated in detail. The Stationers Company, which had helped to administer the licensing system since 1566, was given great powers to control the publication of books and pamphlets and, stimulated by economic incentive, to discover unlicensed printers.

Legal control of the Press was suddenly withdrawn at the abolition of Star Chamber in 1641. All sorts of religious and political enthusiasts seized their chance of publication. During the next two years heaps of topical pamphlets, unlicensed and unregistered, were rushed into print, and the general disorder encouraged some brazen stationers to flout the copyright of books already published. Legitimate trade suffered. Parliament received frequent complaints from the Stationers Company and tried repeatedly to regain control of the Press.

On 29 January 1642, the Commons ordered the Stationers Company not to print or reprint anything without the author's consent and name. (Milton, who maintained in *Areopagitica* that authors and publishers should be answerable to the law for their work, would not have disapproved of this Order.) Two more Orders were passed, one in August 1642, and the other — more potent — in March 1643, as interim measures to curb the liberty of the Press while the Licensing Act was being prepared. This Act seems to have been contemplated as soon as Star Chamber was abolished, and to have been delayed by opposition in Parliament and in the Assembly of Divines as much as by the military 'distractions' used as an excuse in the Order of 1642.

The Stationers Company, which lost money by the growth of unofficial presses, petitioned Parliament in April 1643, to restore control, and the form in which Parliament did so, by the Licensing Order of 14 June, was virtually that of the Star Chamber Decree of 1637.

Parliament's strict and detailed Order was generally obeyed. Milton flouted it, however, and ignored the demands of the Stationers Company, by producing both editions of his first divorce pamphlet unlicensed, unregistered and without a printer's name. The Stationers Company complained specifically about these omissions in a petition to Parliament in August 1644. By then, Milton had already issued his first attack on the Licensing Order: short and sharp, it appears in *A Post-Script* to *The Judgement of Martin Bucer*, which was licensed and printed in July 1644. *Areopagitica*, a quarto of forty pages, deliberately unlicensed and unregistered, was printed four months later. It seems to have attracted little attention at the time, when pleas for liberty by lesser pamphleteers such as John Goodwin and Henry Robinson were more noted.

Attacks on licensing did not change the policy of Parliament, and that policy was often reformulated during Milton's life. When he was himself 'Licenser' of *Mercurius Politicus* in 1651, Milton seems to have acted merely as superintending editor and occasional leader-writer of a government newspaper, and not as that odious official, scorned in *Areopagitica*, the preventive censor.

Areopagitica's indirect influence apparently grew in the struggle for the freedom of the Press during the seventeenth century. Milton's pamphlet was abridged and quoted in others on the subject until the Licensing Act finally lapsed in 1694, twenty years after his death.

There were, however, only eleven complete republications of *Areopagitica* (compared with thirty-six of the tractate *Of Education*) before 1800. When liberalism triumphed in the nineteenth century, *Areopagitica* was acclaimed. Today, in debates on the control of the Press, it is cited as the authoritative work.

3. THE TITLE OF *Areopagitica*

The *Areopagitic Discourse*, or *Areopagiticus*, was the Seventh Oration of Isocrates (436–338 B.C.), who wrote it about 355 B.C. The most famous teacher of rhetoric in his day, Isocrates was unable to speak in public because of his physical and nervous weakness, and so he composed his orations to be read. These highly polished speeches, written at Athens, were circulated throughout Greece.

Like the *Areopagitic Discourse*, Milton's *Areopagitica* is written in the form of a speech to be read, not spoken, and its words simulate those of a private citizen who, at a critical time, pleads for a change of policy by the Athenian parliament.

Isocrates urged the popular assembly of Athens to restore to the Court of Areopagus powers which had lapsed. The Court had formerly influenced religious, moral and political affairs, but its jurisdiction had shrunk and, when Isocrates wrote, it dealt with trivial matters only. (The *Areopagitic Discourse*, like *Areopagitica*, failed to achieve its political aim.)

Milton's purpose is remarkably different from that of Isocrates: the Greek pleaded for control, whereas the Englishman pleads for liberty. Perhaps the title, *Areopagitica*, is intended as a reminder not only of the form of the Greek rhetorician's work, but also of the substance of St. Paul's speech before the Court of Areopagus in Acts 17: 18–34. St. Paul's attack on religious conformity, and his insistence on man's need for freedom to seek God, brings his speech close in spirit to Milton's *Areopagitica*.

4. SYNOPSIS OF *Areopagitica*

Page 13–16 Introduction.

Page 16–24 Part One: *Who started censorship?* ('The inventors of it will be those whom ye will be loath to own.')
Books preserve wisdom, and to kill a good book is to kill reason. We should therefore be careful how we control books. Let us look at the history of censorship.

(*a*) *Greece*
 i. In Athens, prohibited writings were either blasphemous (Protagoras) or libellous (the Older Comedy). The comic dramatists (Aristophanes) could be read, although performance was censored. Philosophers were free.
 ii. In Sparta, literature was not appreciated, and so censorship was unnecessary.

(*b*) *Rome*
 i. *Pagan.* At first the Romans were unliterary. Later, only libel and blasphemy were punished, not philosophy (Lucretius) or

satire (Horace) or outspokenness (Catullus)
or history (Livy). (The banishment of Ovid
was political.)

ii. *Christian.* Heretics' books were not prohibited until their condemnation by a Council
of about A.D. 400. In the fifteenth century,
Pope Martin V attempted to prevent the
reading of heretical books as a measure against
Reformation (Wycliffe and Hus). Pope Leo X,
the Council of Trent and the Spanish
Inquisition suppressed heretical reading.
Licensing and the giving of Imprimatur
really began then. The Anglican Church
adopted the Roman Catholic system.

Page 24–32 Part Two: *Is reading a good thing?* ('What is to be
thought in general of reading?')

(*a*) *Reading in the Bible*
Moses, Daniel and St. Paul were learned.

(*b*) *Reading in the Early Christian Church*
Julian forbad Christians to study because they
defeated their pagan opponents in argument. The
legend of St. Jerome need not be taken seriously.
Dionysius was directed by God to read any books
he wished and to judge them for himself. God re-
vealed His trust in human discretion to St. Peter
also. (Recently Selden has shown that all opinions
serve the truth.)

(*c*) *God does not compel us to temperance: the Bible
shows this*

i. God gave manna in profusion, for temperate
use.

ii. Solomon says that much reading is tiring,
not wrong.

iii. The magic books of St. Paul's converts were
burnt voluntarily.

(d) *Virtue does not depend on innocence*

(e) *Does infection spread by the reading of heretical books?*

    i. The Bible itself shows blasphemy and evil.
    ii. The Early Fathers do too, in relating error, but they are valuable for learning.
    iii. Error is spread not by the act of reading but by evil men infecting other people.

(f) *Licensing is futile*

It is unnecessary for the wise and useless for the fools. Learned men need all kinds of books, so that error can be refuted. Fools cannot be stopped from holding false doctrines.

Page 32–38   Part Three: *This Order does no good*. ('That this Order avails nothing to the suppressing of scandalous, seditious and libellous books which were mainly intended to be suppressed.')

(a) *Plato only intended censorship for an ideal commonwealth*

His impractical scheme would not work in societies as they really are. If we wanted censorship we should not limit it to printing: why not censor all sorts of arts and amusements and pleasures? We would not know where to stop! Morality is better preserved by good religious and civil education.

(b) *Forced obedience is of no value*

You cannot change a sinful nature by removing opportunities for sin: and, if you could do that, you would remove much of the credit of virtue.

(c) *The present Order is inefficient* (e.g. a Royalist paper is published weekly)

For efficiency:
    i. all previous harmful books should be listed;
    ii. foreign books should be examined at the customs;

iii. partly harmful books should be expurgated;
iv. offending printers should be banned.

You need more officials to conduct the Inquisition
with ruthless efficiency: but unwritten opinion is
sure to spread anyway. A censor's work is bound to
be dull. For a man of taste it would be intolerable.
The present staff seems to be tired of it already.
Such officials will be always ignorant, arbitrary,
insolent or venal.

Page 38–64 Part Four: *This Order will do harm.* ('It will be
primely to the discouragement of all learning and
the stop of truth.')

(*a*) *It lowers a man of learning to the level of a
schoolboy*

(*b*) *It lowers the dignity of the nation*
It:
  i. treats knowledge as if it were a dutiable
     commodity;
  ii. treats the people as if they were frivolous and
      vicious;
  iii. shows no faith in the power of the clergy to
       resist false doctrine.

I myself have seen something of this abroad when I
visited Galileo. It is pure prelacy. It makes people
idle in finding truth for themselves and too apt to
rely on the clergy who, not having to meet attacks
on religion, will grow complacent.

(*c*) *Licensing hinders men in their quest for truth*
England is a lively nation, leader of the Reformation throughout Europe. Even under military
threat, Londoners continue the search for truth.
Argument is healthy: let us allow every variety of
opinion. We are on the verge of a national revival.
Parliament's humane control has encouraged
freedom of thought. Let Truth and Falsehood
contend, so that Truth may prevail; she needs no
protection. A rigid external conformity is dead and

dull: a Church ought to have many varieties in it.
We cannot even be sure that the Holy Spirit speaks
exclusively through the Church.

(d) The sensible regulation of printing is not objectionable

This licensing is a revival of tyranny introduced
through the underhand persuasion of the book-
trade. To redress the wrong would be a deed worthy
of Parliament.

II. *AREOPAGITICA*

So long as tyrannies exist, *Areopagitica* will be topical. It
is now regarded, and quoted in Parliament, as the definitive
work on censorship. No more passionate, sincere and noble
plea has yet been written for the liberty of men to print, within
reasonable limits and on their own responsibility, whatever they
wish.

In many countries, men are denied this freedom. We, more
fortunate, should wake up to the fact that there is yet no chance
of this liberty, which we take for granted, becoming world-wide.
Tyrannical governments cannot, because of their nature, allow
freedom of expression. The need to win this freedom for all men
is part of the supreme political challenge of our age. *Areopagitica*
— with its longing for England to lead the world — reminds us
of our good fortune and calls us to free those who cannot print
what they please.

Milton was one of the first writers in his age, which rang with
cries for toleration, to demand this particular freedom. Repression had hurt him personally and, like the rest of his general
demands, the one he voices in *Areopagitica* arose from his own
need deeply felt. *Of Education* and *Areopagitica* are discussions of
what he calls 'domestic or private' liberties. The subject of
Areopagitica is 'the power of free philosophising'. Reviewing his
prose of this period, Milton later recalls in his Latin work
Defensio Secunda:

'Finally, on the subject of the liberation of the Press, so that
the judgement of the true and the false, what should be published and what suppressed, should not be in the hands of a
few men, and these mostly unlearned and of common capacity,
erected into a censorship over books — an agency through
which no one almost either can or will send into the light anything that is above the vulgar taste — on this subject, in the
form of an express oration, I wrote my *Areopagitica*.'

Milton uses the form of a classical oration with masterly ease.
His technique is the fruit of deep-rooted study. *Areopagitica*, as
J. H. Hanford says, 'conforms to all the principles of oratory laid
down by Quintilian and embodied in Demosthenes and Cicero.'

In our age, when oratory has shrunk to fit microphones and television cameras, the form of *Areopagitica* may seem cumbrous and the construction tiresomely elaborate. Milton's many allusions, too, are likely to have lost, in the corroding years, their power to excite. They were intended to disturb and arouse the mind with a tang of immediate response, but few of them do that now. The sharp point that they used to have, when readers were more scholarly, cannot be fully restored by notes.

What still immediately appeals to us, however, is the intensity of *Areopagitica*. Alarmed at the menace of modern propaganda, we are stirred by the confidence that Milton declares in truth's supreme power. Appalled by the morals of our time, we respond to the belief he proclaims in the worth of living nobly. His fervour blazes out in passages of majestic utterance that have rightly become anthology pieces: in them, trumpet-tongued rhetoric declares the grandeur of humanity. His plea, inspired by his anxiety about the developments he saw in Church and State, sounds out today with a ringing sincerity unmuted by three centuries.

Only a detailed study of *Areopagitica* as a whole, however, can reveal the extraordinary scope of Milton's achievement. Variety of tone is no less remarkable, in this speech, than variety of substance. Sometimes he persuades calmly in a voice of cool reason:

> 'The Christian faith, for that was once a schism, is not unknown to have spread all over Asia, ere any gospel or epistle was seen in writing. If the amendment of manners be aimed at, look into Italy and Spain, whether those places be one scruple the better, the honester, the wiser, the chaster, since all the inquisitional rigour that hath been executed upon books.'

Sometimes a tone of satire jibes in mockery:

> 'A wealthy man, addicted to his pleasure and to his profits, finds religion to be a traffic so entangled, and of so many piddling accounts, that of all mysteries he cannot skill to keep a stock going upon that trade.'

Then a dignified tone of heartfelt fervour rings out:

> 'Behold now this vast city: a city of refuge, the mansion house of liberty, encompassed and surrounded with his protection.'

Later, an agonized voice, smarting with regret, exclaims:

> 'How many other things might be tolerated in peace, and left
> to conscience, had we but charity, and were it not the chief
> stronghold of our hypocrisy to be ever judging one another!'

Regret is immediately barbed with scorn:

> 'I fear yet this iron yoke of outward conformity hath left a
> slavish print upon our necks; the ghost of a linen decency yet
> haunts us.'

Milton alters his tone again and again throughout the speech,
matching sound to sense with poetic skill.

Rightly and inevitably we consider Milton's prose as a poetic
performance. *Areopagitica* shows the writer's mind creating
patterns of thought and sound which need the cadences of the
human voice. Sometimes, phrases that look tortuous reveal their
meaning directly to the ear. Often, long straggling sentences,
that drag clause after clause across the pages of *Areopagitica*,
leap, when they are read aloud, into articulated form.

Our efforts to understand the details of the poet's prose are
amply repaid by the vigour and variety of this accomplished,
fervent oratory: it brings to life the rugged power of Milton's
vast and thrusting mind.

Areopagitica

FOR THE LIBERTY OF UNLICENSED PRINTING

THEY, who to states and governors of the Commonwealth direct their speech, High Court of Parliament, or, (wanting such access in a private condition), write that which they foresee may advance the public good; I suppose them, as at the beginning of no mean endeavour, not a little altered and moved inwardly in their minds: some with doubt of what will be the success, others with fear of what will be the censure; some with hope, others with confidence of what they have to speak. And me perhaps each of these dispositions, as the subject was whereon I entered, may have at other times variously affected; and likely might in these foremost expressions now also disclose which of them swayed most, but that the very attempt of this address thus made, and the thought of whom it hath recourse to, hath got the power within me to a passion, far more welcome than incidental to a preface.

Which though I stay not to confess ere any ask, I shall be blameless, if it be no other than the joy and gratulation which it brings to all who wish and promote their country's liberty; whereof this whole discourse proposed will be a certain testimony, if not a trophy. For this is not the liberty which we can hope, that no grievance ever should arise in the Commonwealth — that let no man in this world expect; but when complaints are freely heard, deeply considered and speedily reformed, then is the utmost bound of civil liberty attained that wise men look for. To which if I now manifest by the very sound of this which I shall utter, that we are already in good part arrived, and yet from such a steep disadvantage of tyranny

---

1 *states:* heads.   2 *wanting:* lacking.   3 *in a private condition:* as private individuals.   5 *altered:* disturbed.   7 *success:* result.   *censure:* opinion.   14 *passion:* excitement.   16 *I stay not ... ask:* I readily confess.   20 *trophy:* sign of success.   27 *yet:* even.   *steep:* perilous.

and superstition grounded into our principles as was beyond
the manhood of a Roman recovery, it will be attributed first, as
is most due, to the strong assistance of God our deliverer, next
to your faithful guidance and undaunted wisdom, Lords and
Commons of England. Neither is it in God's esteem the
diminution of His glory, when honourable things are spoken of
good men and worthy magistrates; which if I now first should
begin to do, after so fair a progress of your laudable deeds, and
such a long obligement upon the whole realm to your indefatig-
able virtues, I might be justly reckoned among the tardiest and
the unwillingest of them that praise ye.

Nevertheless there being three principal things without
which all praising is but courtship and flattery: first, when that
only is praised which is solidly worth praise; next, when
greatest likelihoods are brought that such things are truly and
really in those persons to whom they are ascribed; the other,
when he who praises, by showing that such his actual persuasion is of whom he writes, can demonstrate that he flatters not;
the former two of these I have heretofore endeavoured, rescuing the employment from him who went about to impair your
merits with a trivial and malignant encomium; the latter, as be-
longing chiefly to mine own acquittal, that whom I so extolled I
did not flatter, hath been reserved opportunely to this occasion.

For he who freely magnifies what hath been nobly done, and
fears not to declare as freely what might be done better, gives
ye the best covenant of his fidelity, and that his loyalest
affection and his hope waits on your proceedings. His highest
praising is not flattery, and his plainest advice is a kind of
praising. For though I should affirm and hold by argument
that it would fare better with truth, with learning and the Commonwealth, if one of your published Orders, which I should
name, were called in; yet at the same time it could not but much
redound to the lustre of your mild and equal government,

1 *grounded into our principles:* undermining our civil and religious
principles. 2 *the manhood ... recovery:* the power of Rome to recover
from. 9 *obligement upon:* obligation owed by. 20 *went about:* sought.
33 *equal:* equitable.

whenas private persons are hereby animated to think ye better
pleased with public advice, than other statists have been
delighted heretofore with public flattery. And men will then
see what difference there is between the magnanimity of a
triennial parliament, and that jealous haughtiness of prelates
and cabin counsellors that usurped of late, when as they shall
observe ye in the midst of your victories and successes more
gently brooking written exceptions against a voted Order than
other courts, which had produced nothing worth memory but
the weak ostentation of wealth, would have endured the least
signified dislike at any sudden proclamation.

If I should thus far presume upon the meek demeanour of
your civil and gentle greatness, Lords and Commons, as what
your published Order hath directly said, that to gainsay, I
might defend myself with ease, if any should accuse me of
being new or insolent, did they but know how much better I
find ye esteem it to imitate the old and elegant humanity of
Greece, than the barbaric pride of a Hunnish and Norwegian
stateliness. And out of those ages, to whose polite wisdom and
letters we owe that we are not yet Goths and Jutlanders, I
could name him who from his private house wrote that discourse to the parliament of Athens, that persuades them to
change the form of democracy which was then established.
Such honour was done in those days to men who professed the
study of wisdom and eloquence, not only in their own country,
but in other lands, that cities and signiories heard them gladly
and with great respect, if they had aught in public to admonish
the state. Thus did Dion Prusaeus, a stranger and a private
orator, counsel the Rhodians against a former edict; and I
abound with other like examples, which to set here would be
superfluous.

But if from the industry of a life wholly dedicated to studious
labours, and those natural endowments haply not the worst for

1 *whenas:* when. 2 *statists:* statesmen. 6 *cabin:* cabinet. 8 *brooking:* tolerating. 13 *civil:* civilized. 16 *new:* revolutionary. 17 *humanity:* refinement. 19 *stateliness:* overbearing manner. 20 *yet:* still.
26 *cities:* republics. *signiories:* districts under a ruler.

two and fifty degrees of northern latitude, so much must be
derogated as to count me not equal to any of those who had this
privilege, I would obtain to be thought not so inferior as yourselves are superior to the most of them who received their
counsel: and how far you excel them, be assured, Lords and
Commons, there can no greater testimony appear, than when
your prudent spirit acknowledges and obeys the voice of
reason from what quarter soever it be heard speaking; and
renders ye as willing to repeal any Act of your own setting
forth as any set forth by your predecessors.

If ye be thus resolved, as it were injury to think ye were not,
I know not what should withhold me from presenting ye with
a fit instance wherein to show both that love of truth which ye
eminently profess, and that uprightness of your judgment
which is not wont to be partial to yourselves, by judging over
again that Order which ye have ordained to regulate printing:
— that no book, pamphlet or paper shall be henceforth printed,
unless the same be first approved and licensed by such, or at
least one of such, as shall be thereto appointed. For that part
which preserves justly every man's copy to himself, or provides
for the poor, I touch not, only wish they be not made pretences
to abuse and persecute honest and painful men, who offend not
in either of these particulars. But that other clause of licensing
books, which we thought had died with his brother quadragesimal and matrimonial when the prelates expired, I shall
now attend with such a homily as shall lay before ye, first, the
inventors of it to be those whom ye will be loth to own; next,
what is to be thought in general of reading, whatever sort the
books be; and that this Order avails nothing to the suppressing
of scandalous, seditious, and libellous books, which were
mainly intended to be suppressed; last, that it will be primely to

2 *derogated:* subtracted. *this privilege:* the right to 'admonish the
state'. 3 *I would obtain to be:* I would like to succeed in being.
20 *copy:* copyright. 22 *painful:* painstaking. 24 *quadragesimal:* the
lenten licence, by which a bishop gave dispensation from fasting.
25 *matrimonial:* the marriage licence (unlike the modern document of
name), by which a bishop gave exemption from the publication of the
banns.

the discouragement of all learning, and the stop of truth, not only by disexercising and blunting our abilities in what we know already, but by hindering and cropping the discovery that might be yet further made both in religious and civil wisdom.

I deny not but that it is of greatest concernment in the Church and Commonwealth to have a vigilant eye how books demean themselves as well as men; and thereafter to confine, imprison, and do sharpest justice on them as malefactors. For books are not absolutely dead things, but do contain a potency of life in them to be as active as that soul was whose progeny they are; nay, they do preserve as in a vial the purest efficacy and extraction of that living intellect that bred them. I know they are as lively, and as vigorously productive, as those fabulous dragon's teeth; and, being sown up and down, may chance to spring up armed men. And yet, on the other hand, unless wariness be used, as good almost kill a man as kill a good book. Who kills a man kills a reasonable creature, God's image; but he who destroys a good book, kills reason itself, kills the image of God, as it were in the eye. Many a man lives a burden to the earth; but a good book is the precious life-blood of a master spirit, embalmed and treasured up on purpose to a life beyond life. 'Tis true, no age can restore a life, whereof perhaps there is no great loss; and revolutions of ages do not oft recover the loss of a rejected truth, for the want of which whole nations fare the worse.

We should be wary therefore what persecution we raise against the living labours of public men, how we spill that seasoned life of man preserved and stored up in books; since we see a kind of homicide may be thus committed, sometimes a martyrdom, and, if it extend to the whole impression, a kind of massacre; whereof the execution ends not in the slaying of an elemental life, but strikes at that ethereal and fifth essence, the

20 *as it were in the eye:* as reflected directly in the human mind. 28 *spill:* destroy.   31 *impression:* printing.   32 *an elemental life:* a life depending on the four elements which were believed to compose all earthly creation.

c

breath of reason itself; slays an immortality rather than a life. But lest I should be condemned of introducing licence, while I oppose licensing, I refuse not the pains to be so much historical as will serve to show what hath been done by ancient and famous commonwealths against this disorder, till the very time that this project of licensing crept out of the Inquisition, was catched up by our prelates, and hath caught some of our presbyters.

In Athens, where books and wits were ever busier than in any other part of Greece, I find but only two sorts of writings which the magistrate cared to take notice of: those either blasphemous and atheistical, or libellous. Thus the books of Protagoras were by the judges of Areopagus commanded to be burnt, and himself banished the territory, for a discourse begun with his confessing not to know *whether there were gods, or whether not*. And against defaming, it was decreed that none should be traduced by name, as was the manner of Vetus Comoedia, whereby we may guess how they censured libelling. And this course was quick enough, as Cicero writes, to quell both the desperate wits of other atheists, and the open way of defaming, as the event showed.

Of other sects and opinions, though tending to voluptuousness and the denying of divine providence, they took no heed. Therefore we do not read that either Epicurus, or that libertine school of Cyrene, or what the Cynic impudence uttered, was ever questioned by the laws. Neither is it recorded that the writings of those old comedians were suppressed, though the acting of them were forbid; and that Plato commended the reading of Aristophanes, the loosest of them all, to his royal scholar Dionysius, is commonly known, and may be excused, if holy Chrysostom, as is reported, nightly studied so much the same author and had the art to cleanse a scurrilous vehemence into the style of a rousing sermon.

That other leading city of Greece, Lacedaemon, considering

2 *licence:* excessive liberty.   6 *Inquisition:* Roman Catholic tribunal for the suppression of heresy.   19 *quick:* vigorous.   *quell:* kill.
21 *event:* result.   34 *Lacedaemon:* Sparta.

that Lycurgus their lawgiver was so addicted to elegant learning
as to have been the first that brought out of Ionia the scattered
works of Homer, and sent the poet Thales from Crete to
prepare and mollify the Spartan surliness with his smooth
songs and odes, the better to plant among them law and civility,
it is to be wondered how museless and unbookish they were,
minding nought but the feats of war. There needed no licensing
of books among them, for they disliked all but their own laconic
apothegms, and took a slight occasion to chase Archilochus out
of their city, perhaps for composing in a higher strain than
their own soldierly ballads and roundels could reach to. Or if it
were for his broad verses, they were not therein so cautious but
they were as dissolute in their promiscuous conversing; whence
Euripides affirms in *Andromache* that their women were all
unchaste. Thus much may give us light after what sort books
were prohibited among the Greeks.

The Romans also, for many ages trained up only to a military
roughness, resembling most of the Lacedaemonian guise, knew
of learning little but what their twelve tables and the pontific
college with their augurs and flamens taught them in religion
and law, so unacquainted with other learning that when
Carneades and Critolaus with the Stoic Diogenes, coming
ambassadors to Rome, took thereby occasion to give the city a
taste of their philosophy, they were suspected for seducers by
no less a man than Cato the Censor, who moved it in the Senate
to dismiss them speedily, and to banish all such Attic babblers
out of Italy. But Scipio and others of the noblest senators with-
stood him and his old Sabine austerity; honoured and admired

2 *Ionia:* a country of Asia Minor. 5 *civility:* refinement. 6 *museless:*
uncivilized. 8 *laconic:* i. sententious *and* ii. Spartan. 9 *apothegms:* pithy maxims. 11 *roundels:* songs with choruses. 12 *broad:*
coarse. 12–13 *they were not therein . . . dissolute:* their caution in this
matter did not prevent their being just as dissolute. *conversing:*
manner of life. 15 *give us light after what sort:* show us how.
19 *their twelve tables:* the legal code of Rome, memorized by Roman
schoolboys. *pontific college:* overseers of Roman worship. 20 *augurs:*
priests who declared omens. *flamens:* priests of the sacrificial fires.
24 *seducers:* corrupters. 25 *moved it:* proposed a motion. 26 *Attic:*
Greek.

the men; and the censor himself at last, in his old age, fell to the study of that whereof before he was so scrupulous. And yet, at the same time, Naevius and Plautus, the first Latin comedians, had filled the city with all the borrowed scenes of Menander and Philemon. Then began to be considered there also what was to be done to libellous books and authors; for Naevius was quickly cast into prison for his unbridled pen, and released by the tribunes upon his recantation; we read also that libels were burnt, and the makers punished by Augustus. The like severity, no doubt, was used if aught were impiously written against their esteemed gods.

Except in these two points, how the world went in books the magistrate kept no reckoning. And therefore Lucretius without impeachment versifies his Epicurism to Memmius, and had the honour to be set forth the second time by Cicero, so great a father of the commonwealth; although himself disputes against that opinion in his own writings. Nor was the satirical sharpness or naked plainness of Lucilius, or Catullus, or Flaccus, by any order prohibited. And for matters of state, the story of Titus Livius, though it extolled that part which Pompey held, was not therefore suppressed by Octavius Caesar of the other faction. But that Naso was by him banished in his old age for the wanton poems of his youth, was but a mere covert of state over some secret cause; and besides, the books were neither banished nor called in. From hence we shall meet with little else but tyranny in the Roman empire, that we may not marvel if not so often bad as good books were silenced. I shall therefore deem to have been large enough in producing what among the ancients was punishable to write; save only which, all other arguments were free to treat on.

By this time the emperors were become Christians, whose discipline in this point I do not find to have been more severe than what was formerly in practice. The books of those whom

14 *impeachment:* hindrance. 15 *set forth:* edited. 19 *the story of Titus Livius:* the History of Rome by Livy. 23–4 *covert of state over:* politic pretext to hide. 28 *deem to have been large:* consider myself to have expatiated. 30 *arguments were free to treat on:* themes could be treated freely.

they took to be grand heretics were examined, refuted, and condemned in the general councils; and not till then were prohibited, or burnt, by authority of the emperor. As for the writings of heathen authors, unless they were plain invectives against Christianity, as those óf Porphyrius and Proclus, they met with no interdict that can be cited, till about the year 400 in a Carthaginian Council, wherein bishops themselves were forbid to read the books of Gentiles, but heresies they might read: while others long before them, on the contrary, scrupled more the books of heretics than of Gentiles. And that the primitive councils and bishops were wont only to declare what books were not commendable, passing no further, but leaving it to each one's conscience to read or to lay by, till after the year 800, is observed already by Padre Paolo, the great unmasker of the Trentine council.

After which time, the popes of Rome, engrossing what they pleased of political rule into their own hands, extended their dominion over men's eyes, as they had before over their judgments, burning and prohibiting to be read what they fancied not; yet sparing in their censures, and the books not many which they so dealt with: till Martin V, by his bull, not only prohibited, but was the first that excommunicated the reading of heretical books; for about that time Wycliffe and Hus, growing terrible, were they who first drove the papal court to a stricter policy of prohibiting. Which course Leo X and his successors followed, until the Council of Trent and the Spanish Inquisition engendering together brought forth or perfected those catalogues and expurging indexes, that rake through the entrails of many an old good author, with a violation worse than any could be offered to his tomb. Nor did they stay in matters heretical, but any subject that was not to their palate they either condemned in a prohibition, or had it straight into the new purgatory of an index.

9 *scrupled more:* scrupled more about. 12 *passing:* going. 13 *lay by:* lay aside unread. 16 *which time:* A.D. 800. *engrossing:* seizing. 22 *excommunicated the reading:* punished the reading with excommunication. 27 *catalogues:* lists of books forbidden by the pope. 28 *expurging indexes:* lists of books that could not be printed without expurgations. 32 *straight:* at once. *purgatory:* place of cleansing.

To fill up the measure of encroachment, their last invention
was to ordain that no book, pamphlet, or paper should be
printed (as if St. Peter had bequeathed them the keys of the
press also out of paradise) unless it were approved and licensed
under the hands of two or three glutton friars. For example:

> Let the Chancellor Cini be pleased to see if in this present
> work be contained aught that may withstand the
> printing,
> > Vincent Rabatta, Vicar of Florence.

> I have seen this present work, and find nothing athwart
> the Catholic faith and good manners; in witness whereof
> I have given, &c.
> > Nicolò Cini, Chancellor of Florence.

> Attending the precedent relation, it is allowed that this
> present work of Davanzati may be printed,
> > Vincent Rabatta, &c.

> It may be printed, July 15.
> > Friar Simon Mompei d'Amelia, Chancellor of
> > the Holy Office in Florence.

Sure they have a conceit, if he of the bottomless pit had not
long since broke prison, that this quadruple exorcism would
bar him down! I fear their next design will be to get into their
custody the licensing of that which they say Claudius intended,*
but went not through with. Vouchsafe to see another of their
forms, the Roman stamp:

> Imprimatur, If it seem good to the reverend master of
> the Holy Palace,   Belcastro, Viceregent.

> Imprimatur, Friar Nicolò Rodolphi, Master of the Holy
> Palace.

---

* Quo veniam daret flatum crepitumque ventris in convivio
emittendi. *Sueton. in Claudio.* (Milton's footnote.)

9 *Vicar:* delegate.   20 *conceit:* idea *and* arrogance.   *he of the bottomless pit:* Satan.   21 *exorcism:* binding by oath.   26 *Imprimatur:* let it be
printed.

Sometimes five imprimaturs are seen together dialoguewise
in the piazza of one title-page, complimenting and ducking
each to other with their shaven reverences, whether the author
who stands by in perplexity at the foot of his epistle, shall to the
press or to the sponge. These are the pretty responsories, these
are the dear antiphonies that so bewitched of late our prelates
and their chaplains with the goodly echo they made; and
besotted us to the gay imitation of a lordly imprimatur, one
from Lambeth House, another from the west end of Paul's; so
apishly Romanizing that the word of command still was set
down in Latin; as if the learned grammatical pen that wrote it
would cast no ink without Latin; or perhaps, as they thought,
because no vulgar tongue was worthy to express the pure
conceit of an imprimatur; but rather, as I hope, for that our
English, the language of men ever famous and foremost in the
achievements of liberty, will not easily find servile letters
enough to spell such a dictatory presumption English.

And thus ye have the inventors and the original of book-
licensing ripped up and drawn as lineally as any pedigree. We
have it not, that can be heard of, from any ancient state, or
polity or church; nor by any statute left us by our ancestors,
elder or later; nor from the modern custom of any reformed
city or church abroad; but from the most anti-christian
council and the most tyrannous inquisition that ever inquired.
Till then books were ever as freely admitted into the world as
any other birth; the issue of the brain was no more stifled than
the issue of the womb: no envious Juno sat cross-legged over
the nativity of any man's intellectual offspring; but if it proved
a monster, who denies but that it was justly burnt, or sunk into
the sea? But that a book, in worse condition than a peccant

2 *piazza:* meeting-place. *ducking:* bowing. 3 *shaven reverences:*
tonsured heads. 5 *responsories:* parts of the service that contain re-
sponses. 6 *antiphonies:* chants sung by alternating voices. 9 *Lambeth
House:* Lambeth Palace, London residence of the Archibishop of
Canterbury. *the west end of Paul's:* the Bishop of London's palace,
which used to be in the precincts of St. Paul's cathedral. 13 *no vulgar
tongue:* no language but that of the educated, which was Latin.
17 *dictatory:* dictatorial. 19 *ripped up:* torn open. 21 *polity:* form
of civil government. 30 *peccant:* sinning.

soul, should be to stand before a jury ere it be born to the
world, and undergo yet in darkness the judgment of Radamanth and his colleagues, ere it can pass the ferry backward
into light, was never heard before — till that mysterious
iniquity, provoked and troubled at the first entrance of
Reformation, sought out new limbos and new hells wherein
they might include our books also within the number of their
damned. And this was the rare morsel so officiously snatched
up, and so ill-favouredly imitated by our inquisiturient bishops,
and the attendant minorites their chaplains! That ye like not
now these most certain authors of this licensing order, and that
all sinister intention was far distant from your thoughts when
ye were importuned the passing of it, all men who know the
integrity of your actions, and how ye honour truth, will clear
ye readily.

But some will say, What though the inventors were bad, the
thing for all that may be good? It may be so; yet if that thing
be no such deep invention, but obvious, and easy for any man
to light on, and yet best and wisest commonwealths through all
ages and occasions have forborne to use it, and falsest seducers
and oppressors of men were the first who took it up, and to no
other purpose but to obstruct and hinder the first approach of
reformation — I am of those who believe it will be a harder
alchymy than Lullius ever knew, to sublimate any good use out
of such an invention. Yet this only is what I request to gain
from this reason, that it may be held a dangerous and suspicious
fruit, as certainly it deserves, for the tree that bore it, until I
can dissect one by one the properties it has. But I have first to
finish, as was propounded, what is to be thought in general of
reading books, whatever sort they be, and whether be more the
benefit or the harm that thence proceeds?

Not to insist upon the examples of Moses, Daniel and Paul,
who were skilful in all the learning of the Egyptians, Chaldeans

4–5 *that mysterious iniquity:* the Church of Rome. 6 *limbos:* borders
of hell. 9 *ill-favouredly:* foully. *inquisiturient bishops:* bishops longing to be inquisitors. 10 *minorites:* friars. 24 *alchymy:* chemistry.
sublimate: extract. 26 *reason:* argument. 27 *for:* because of.

and Greeks, (which could not probably be without reading
their books of all sorts; in Paul especially, who thought it no
defilement to insert into holy scripture the sentences of three
Greek poets, and one of them a tragedian); the question was
notwithstanding sometimes controverted among the primitive
doctors, but with great odds on that side which affirmed it both
lawful and profitable. As was then evidently perceived, when
Julian the Apostate and subtlest enemy to our faith made a
decree forbidding Christians the study of heathen learning: for,
said he, they wound us with our own weapons, and with our
own arts and sciences they overcome us. And indeed the
Christians were put so to their shifts by this crafty means and
so much in danger to decline into all ignorance, that the two
Appolinarii were fain, as a man may say, to coin all the seven
liberal sciences out of the Bible, reducing it into divers forms
of orations, poems, dialogues, even to the calculating of a new
Christian grammar. But, saith the historian Socrates, the
providence of God provided better than the industry of
Apollinarius and his son by taking away that illiterate law with
the life of him who devised it. So great an injury they then held
it to be deprived of Hellenic learning; and thought it a persecution more undermining, and secretly decaying the Church,
than the open cruelty of Decius or Diocletian.

And perhaps it was the same politic drift that the devil
whipped St. Jerome in a lenten dream, for reading Cicero; or
else it was a phantasm bred by the fever which had then seized
him. For had an angel been his discipliner, unless it were for
dwelling too much upon Ciceronianisms, and had chastised the
reading, not the vanity, it had been plainly partial: first, to
correct him for grave Cicero, and not for scurril Plautus whom
he confesses to have been reading not long before; next, to
correct him only, and let so many more ancient fathers wax old
in those pleasant and florid studies without the lash of such a
tutoring apparition. Insomuch that Basil teaches how some

3 *sentences:* wise sayings. 5 *controverted:* discussed. 6 *odds:* superiority. 8 *Apostate:* deserter. 12 *shifts:* devices. 13 *to decline:* of de-
clining. 30 *scurril:* scurrilous.

good use may be made of *Margites*, a sportful poem, not now extant, writ by Homer; and why not then of *Morgante*, an Italian romance much to the same purpose?

But if it be agreed we shall be tried by visions, there is a vision recorded by Eusebius, far ancienter than this tale of Jerome to the nun Eustochium, and, besides, has nothing of a fever in it. Dionysius Alexandrinus was, about the year 240, a person of great name in the Church for piety and learning, who had wont to avail himself much against heretics by being conversant in their books; until a certain presbyter laid it scrupulously to his conscience, how he durst venture himself among those defiling volumes. The worthy man, loth to give offence, fell into a new debate with himself what was to be thought; when suddenly a vision sent from God (it is his own epistle that so avers it) confirmed him in these words: 'Read any books whatever come to thy hands, for thou art sufficient both to judge aright and to examine each matter.' To this revelation he assented the sooner, as he confesses, because it was answerable to that of the Apostle to the Thessalonians: 'Prove all things, hold fast that which is good.' And he might have added another remarkable saying of the same author: 'To the pure all things are pure'; not only meats and drinks, but all kind of knowledge whether of good or evil: the knowledge cannot defile, nor consequently the books, if the will and conscience be not defiled.

For books are as meats and viands are: some of good, some of evil substance; and yet God in that unapocryphal vision said without exception, 'Rise, Peter, kill and eat,' leaving the choice to each man's discretion. Wholesome meats to a vitiated stomach differ little or nothing from unwholesome; and best books to a naughty mind are not unappliable to occasions of evil. Bad meats will scarce breed good nourishment in the healthiest concoction; but herein the difference is of bad books, that they to a discreet and judicious reader serve in many

had: was. 19 *answerable to:* consistent with. *the Apostle:* St. Paul. 20 *prove:* test. 27 *unapocryphal:* true. 31 *naughty:* evil.

respects to discover, to confute, to forewarn, and to illustrate. Whereof what better witness can ye expect I should produce than one of your own now sitting in Parliament, the chief of learned men reputed in this land, Mr. Selden; whose volume of natural and national laws proves, not only by great authorities brought together, but by exquisite reasons and theorems almost mathematically demonstrative, that all opinions — yea, errors! — known, read, and collated, are of main service and assistance toward the speedy attainment of what is truest. I conceive, therefore, that when God did enlarge the universal diet of man's body, saving ever the rules of temperance, He then also, as before, left arbitrary the dieting and repasting of our minds; as wherein every mature man might have to exercise his own leading capacity.

How great a virtue is temperance, how much of moment through the whole life of man! Yet God commits the managing so great a trust, without particular law or prescription, wholly to the demeanour of every grown man. And therefore when He himself tabled the Jews from heaven, that omer, which was every man's daily portion of manna, is computed to have been more than might have well sufficed the heartiest feeder thrice as many meals. For those actions which enter into a man, rather than issue out of him, and therefore defile not, God uses not to captivate under a perpetual childhood of prescription, but trusts him with the gift of reason to be his own chooser; there were but little work left for preaching, if law and compulsion should grow so fast upon those things which heretofore were governed only by exhortation. Solomon informs us that much reading is a weariness to the flesh, but neither he, nor other inspired author, tells us that such or such reading is unlawful: yet certainly had God thought good to limit us herein, it had been much more expedient to have told us what was unlawful than what was wearisome. As for the burning of those Ephesian books by St. Paul's converts, 'tis replied the books

1 *discover:* reveal. 6 *exquisite:* careful. *theorems:* theories. 11 *saving:* excepting. 12 *repasting:* feeding. 18 *demeanour:* behaviour. 19 *tabled:* gave laws. *omer:* Hebrew measure of capacity.

were magic; the Syriac so renders them. It was a private act, a voluntary act, and leaves us to a voluntary imitation: the men in remorse burnt those books which were their own; the magistrate by this example is not appointed; these men practised the books, another might perhaps have read them in some sort usefully.

Good and evil we know in the field of this world grow up together almost inseparably; and the knowledge of good is so involved and interwoven with the knowledge of evil, and in so many cunning resemblances hardly to be discerned, that those confused seeds which were imposed on Psyche as an incessant labour to cull out, and sort asunder, were not more intermixed. It was from out the rind of one apple tasted, that the knowledge of good and evil, as two twins cleaving together, leaped forth into the world. And perhaps this is that doom which Adam fell into of knowing good and evil; that is to say, of knowing good by evil. As, therefore, the state of man now is, what wisdom can there be to choose, what continence to forbear, without the knowledge of evil? He that can apprehend and consider vice with all her baits and seeming pleasures, and yet abstain, and yet distinguish, and yet prefer that which is truly better, he is the true warfaring Christian.

I cannot praise a fugitive and cloistered virtue, unexercised and unbreathed, that never sallies out and sees her adversary, but slinks out of the race, where that immortal garland is to be run for not without dust and heat. Assuredly we bring not innocence into the world, we bring impurity much rather; that which purifies us is trial, and trial is by what is contrary. That virtue therefore which is but a youngling in the contemplation of evil, and knows not the utmost that vice promises to her followers, and rejects it, is but a blank virtue, not a pure; her whiteness is but an excremental whiteness. Which was the reason why our sage and serious poet Spenser, whom I dare be known to think a better teacher than Scotus or Aquinas,

1 *Syriac:* Aramaic language. 4 *practised the books:* used the books to help them to practise magic. 18 *to choose:* in choosing. 31 *blank:* colourless. 32 *excremental:* superficial.

describing true temperance under the person of Guion, brings
him in with his palmer through the cave of Mammon and the
bower of earthly bliss, that he might see and know, and yet
abstain. Since therefore the knowledge and survey of vice is in
this world so necessary to the constituting of human virtue, and
the scanning of error to the confirmation of truth, how can we
more safely, and with less danger, scout into the regions of sin
and falsity than by reading all manner of tractates and hearing
all manner of reason? And this is the benefit which may be had
of books promiscuously read.

But of the harm that may result hence, three kinds are usually
reckoned. First, is feared the infection that may spread; but
then all human learning and controversy in religious points
must remove out of the world, yea, the Bible itself; for that
ofttimes relates blasphemy not nicely, it describes the carnal
sense of wicked men not unelegantly, it brings in holiest men
passionately murmuring against providence through all the
arguments of Epicurus: in other great disputes it answers
dubiously and darkly to the common reader. And ask a Talmudist what ails the modesty of his marginal Keri, that Moses
and all the prophets cannot persuade him to pronounce the
textual Chetiv. For these causes we all know the Bible itself
put by the papist into the first rank of prohibited books. The
ancientest fathers must be next removed, as Clement of Alexandria, and that Eusebian book of evangelic preparation, trans-
mitting our ears through a hoard of heathenish obscenities to
receive the gospel. Who finds not that Irenaeus, Epiphanius,
Jerome, and others discover more heresies than they well confute, and that oft for heresy which is the truer opinion?

Nor boots it to say for these, and all the heathen writers of
greatest infection, if it must be thought so, with whom is

2 *palmer:* pilgrim. 8 *tractates:* literary works. 10 *promiscuously:*
unrestrictedly. 15 *not nicely:* plainly. 16 *not unelegantly:* elaborately.
19 *Talmudist:* expert in the Talmud (the body of Jewish law and
legend). *Keri:* words written in the margin, to be read instead of forbidden or undesirable ones in the unalterable
text. 22 *Chetiv:* words of Hebrew Scripture. 28 *discover:* reveal.
30 *boots:* avails.

bound up the life of human learning, that they writ in an
unknown tongue, so long as we are sure those languages are
known as well to the worst of men, who are both most able and
most diligent to instil the poison they suck, first into the courts
of princes, acquainting them with the choicest delights and
criticisms of sin. As perhaps did that Petronius whom Nero
called his arbiter, the master of his revels; and that notorious
ribald of Arezzo, dreaded and yet dear to the Italian courtiers.
I name not him, for posterity's sake, whom Henry VIII named
in merriment his vicar of hell. By which compendious way all
the contagion that foreign books can infuse will find a passage
to the people far easier and shorter than an Indian voyage,
though it could be sailed either by the north of Cataio eastward
or of Canada westward, while our Spanish licensing gags the
English press never so severely.

But on the other side, that infection which is from books of
controversy in religion is more doubtful and dangerous to the
learned than to the ignorant; and yet those books must be permitted untouched by the licenser. It will be hard to instance
where any ignorant man hath been ever seduced by papistical
book in English, unless it were commended and expounded to
him by some of that clergy; and indeed all such tractates
whether false or true are as the prophecy of Isaiah was to the
eunuch, not to be understood without a guide. But of our
priests and doctors how many have been corrupted by studying
the comments of Jesuits and Sorbonists, and how fast they
could transfuse that corruption into the people, our experience
is both late and sad. It is not forgot, since the acute and distinct
Arminius was perverted merely by the perusing of a nameless
discourse written at Delft, which at first he took in hand to
confute.

Seeing therefore that those books, and those in great
abundance, which are likeliest to taint both life and doctrine,

6 *criticisms:* subtleties.   9 *for posterity's sake:* because of his descen-
dants.   10 *compendious:* short.   13 *Cataio:* Cathay.   14 *Spanish:*
inquisitorial.   17 *doubtful:* fearful.   26 *Sorbonists:* scholars of the Sor-
bonne, the great theological school in Paris.   28 *distinct:* clear-
headed.   29 *nameless:* anonymous.

cannot be suppressed without the fall of learning and of all ability in disputation, and that these books of either sort are most and soonest catching to the learned, from whom to the common people whatever is heretical or dissolute may quickly be conveyed, and that evil manners are as perfectly learnt without books a thousand other ways which cannot be stopped, and evil doctrine not with books can propagate, except a teacher guide — which he might also do without writing, and so beyond prohibiting — I am not able to unfold how this cautelous enterprise of licensing can be exempted from the number of vain and impossible attempts. And he who were pleasantly disposed could not well avoid to liken it to the exploit of that gallant man who thought to pound up the crows by shutting his park gate.

Besides, another inconvenience: if learned men be the first receivers out of books and dispreaders both of vice and error, how shall the licensers themselves be confided in, unless we can confer upon them, or they assume to themselves above all others in the land, the grace of infallibility and uncorrupted-ness? And again, if it be true that a wise man, like a good refiner, can gather gold out of the drossiest volume, and that a fool will be a fool with the best book — yea, or without book! — there is no reason that we should deprive a wise man of any advantage to his wisdom, while we seek to restrain from a fool that which being restrained will be no hindrance to his folly. For if there should be so much exactness always used to keep that from him which is unfit for his reading, we should, in the judgment of Aristotle not only but of Solomon and of our Saviour, not vouchsafe him good precepts, and by consequence not willingly admit him to good books; as being certain that a wise man will make better use of an idle pamphlet, than a fool will do of sacred scripture.

'Tis next alleged we must not expose ourselves to tempt-ations without necessity, and next to that, not employ our time in vain things. To both these objections one answer will serve,

10 *cautelous:* crafty. 13 *pound:* shut. 16 *dispreaders:* spreaders about.
27 *him:* the fool. 31 *idle:* trifling.

out of the grounds already laid: that to all men such books are
not temptations, nor vanities, but useful drugs and materials
wherewith to temper and compose effective and strong
medicines, which man's life cannot want. The rest, as children
and childish men, who have not the art to qualify and prepare
these working minerals, well may be exhorted to forbear; but
hindered forcibly they cannot be by all the licensing that
sainted Inquisition could ever yet contrive. Which is what I
promised to deliver next: that this Order of licensing conduces
nothing to the end for which it was framed; and hath almost
prevented me by being clear already while thus much hath
been explaining. See the ingenuity of Truth, who, when she
gets a free and willing hand, opens herself faster than the pace
of method and discourse can overtake her!

It was the task which I began with, to show that no nation,
or well instituted state, if they valued books at all, did ever use
this way of licensing; and it might be answered, that this is a
piece of prudence lately discovered. To which I return, that as
it was a thing slight and obvious to think on, so if it had been
difficult to find out, there wanted not among them long since
who suggested such a course; which they not following leave us
a pattern of their judgment, that it was not the not knowing,
but the not approving, which was the cause of their not using
it.

Plato, a man of high authority indeed, but least of all for his
commonwealth, in the book of his Laws, which no city ever yet
received, fed his fancy with making many edicts to his airy
burgomasters, which they who otherwise admire him wish had
been rather buried and excused in the genial cups of an
Academic night-sitting. By which laws he seems to tolerate no
kind of learning but by unalterable decree, consisting most of
practical traditions, to the attainment whereof a library of
smaller bulk than his own dialogues would be abundant. And

4 *want:* do without.   5 *qualify:* moderate.   11 *prevented:* forestalled.
12 *ingenuity:* frankness.   14 *discourse:* reason.   18 *return:* reply.
27 *airy:* imaginary.   28 *burgomasters:* local rulers.   30 *night-sitting:*
drinking party.   31 *but by:* except that permitted by.   32 *practical traditions:* e.g. agriculture.   33 *dialogues:* writings in conversational form.

there also enacts that no poet should so much as read to any private man what he had written, until the judges and law-keepers had seen it and allowed it. But that Plato meant this law peculiarly to that commonwealth which he had imagined, and to no other, is evident. Why was he not else a lawgiver to himself, but a transgressor, and to be expelled by his own magistrates, both for the wanton epigrams and dialogues which he made, and his perpetual reading of Sophron Mimus and Aristophanes, books of grossest infamy; and also for com-mending the latter of them, though he were the malicious libeller of his chief friends, to be read by the tyrant Dionysius, who had little need of such trash to spend his time on? But that he knew this licensing of poems had reference and dependence to many other provisos there set down in his fancied republic, which in this world could have no place; and so neither he himself, nor any magistrate or city, ever imitated that course, which, taken apart from those other collateral injunctions, must needs be vain and fruitless. For if they fell upon one kind of strictness, unless their care were equal to regulate all other things of like aptness to corrupt the mind, that single endeavour they knew would be but a fond labour: to shut and fortify one gate against corruption, and be necessitated to leave others round about wide open.

If we think to regulate printing, thereby to rectify manners, we must regulate our recreations and pastimes, all that is delightful to man. No music must be heard, no song be set or sung, but what is grave and Doric. There must be licensing dancers, that no gesture, motion, or deportment be taught our youth but what by their allowance shall be thought honest; for such Plato was provided of. It will ask more than the work of twenty licensers to examine all the lutes, and violins, and the guitars in every house; they must not be suffered to prattle as they do, but must be licensed what they may say. And who shall silence all the airs and madrigals that whisper softness in

6 *to be expelled:* deserving banishment.   18 *fell upon:* enforced.
21 *fond:* foolish.   27 *Doric:* manly.   29 *honest:* decent.   *for such Plato was provided of:* Plato had provided for all that.

D

chambers? The windows also, and the balconies must be
thought on; there are shrewd books, with dangerous frontis-
pieces, set to sale: who shall prohibit them? shall twenty
licensers? The villages also must have their visitors to inquire
what lectures the bagpipe and the rebeck reads, even to the
ballatry and the gamut of every municipal fiddler; for these are
the countryman's Arcadias and his Monte Mayors.

Next, what more national corruption, for which England
hears ill abroad, than household gluttony? Who shall be the
rectors of our daily rioting? And what shall be done to inhibit
the multitudes that frequent those houses where drunkenness
is sold and harboured? Our garments also should be referred
to the licensing of some more sober workmasters, to see them
cut into a less wanton garb. Who shall regulate all the mixed
conversation of our youth, male and female together, as is the
fashion of this country? Who shall still appoint what shall be
discoursed, what presumed, and no further? Lastly, who shall
forbid and separate all idle resort, all evil company? These
things will be, and must be; but how they shall be least hurtful,
how least enticing, herein consists the grave and governing
wisdom of a state.

To sequester out of the world into Atlantic and Utopian
polities which never can be drawn into use, will not mend our
condition; but to ordain wisely as in this world of evil, in the
midst whereof God hath placed us unavoidably. Nor is it
Plato's licensing of books will do this, which necessarily pulls
along with it so many other kinds of licensing, as will make us all
both ridiculous and weary, and yet frustrate; but those unwritten, or at least unconstraining laws of virtuous education,
religious and civil nurture, which Plato there mentions as the
bonds and ligaments of the commonwealth, the pillars and the
sustainers of every written statute; these they be which will

2 *shrewd:* mischievous.   4 *visitors:* inspectors.   5 *lectures:* sermons.
rebeck: fiddle.   6 *ballatry:* balladry.   *gamut:* range of notes.   *municipal:* of a small country town.   9 *hears:* is heard of.   10 *rioting:*
indulgence.   15 *conversation:* behaviour.   17 *what presumed:* how far
we may go.   22 *sequester:* withdraw.   *Atlantic and Utopian polities:*
perfect, imaginary societies.   28 *frustrate:* it will prove ineffectual.

bear chief sway in such matters as these, when all licensing will
be easily eluded. Impunity and remissness, for certain, are the
bane of a commonwealth; but here the great art lies to discern
in what the law is to bid restraint and punishment, and in what
things persuasion only is to work.

If every action which is good or evil in man at ripe years
were to be under pittance, and prescription, and compulsion,
what were virtue but a name, what praise could be then due to
well-doing, what grammercy to be sober, just, or continent?
Many there be that complain of divine providence for suffering
Adam to transgress. Foolish tongues! When God gave him
reason, He gave him freedom to choose, for reason is but
choosing; he had been else a mere artificial Adam, such an
Adam as he is in the motions. We ourselves esteem not of that
obedience, or love, or gift, which is of force: God therefore left
him free, set before him a provoking object, ever almost in his
eyes; herein consisted his merit, herein the right of his reward,
the praise of his abstinence. Wherefore did He create passions
within us, pleasures round about us, but that these rightly
tempered are the very ingredients of virtue?

They are not skilful considerers of human things, who
imagine to remove sin by removing the matter of sin; for,
besides that it is a huge heap increasing under the very act of
diminishing, though some part of it may for a time be withdrawn from some persons, it cannot from all, in such a universal
thing as books are; and when this is done, yet the sin remains
entire. Though ye take from a covetous man all his treasure, he
has yet one jewel left: ye cannot bereave him of his covetous-
ness. Banish all objects of lust, shut up all youth into the severest
discipline that can be exercised in any hermitage, ye cannot
make them chaste that came not thither so; such great care and
wisdom is required to the right managing of this point. Suppose
we could expel sin by this means; look how much we thus expel

---

3 *to discern:* in discerning.   7 *pittance:* permission.   9 *grammercy
to be:* great thanks for being.   14 *motions:* puppet-shows.   *esteem not:*
do not think highly.   16 *provoking:* enticing.   25 *it cannot from:* it
cannot be withdrawn from.

of sin, so much we expel of virtue: for the matter of them both is the same; remove that, and ye remove them both alike.

This justifies the high providence of God, who, though He commands us temperance, justice, continence, yet pours out before us, even to a profuseness, all desirable things, and gives us minds that can wander beyond all limit and satiety. Why should we then affect a rigour contrary to the manner of God and of nature, by abridging or scanting those means, which books freely permitted are, both to the trial of virtue and the exercise of truth? It would be better done to learn that the law must needs be frivolous which goes to restrain things uncertainly and yet equally working to good and to evil. And were I the chooser, a dram of well-doing should be preferred before many times as much the forcible hindrance of evil-doing. For God sure esteems the growth and completing of one virtuous person more than the restraint of ten vicious.

And albeit whatever thing we hear or see, sitting, walking, travelling, or conversing may be fitly called our book, and is of the same effect that writings are, yet grant the thing to be prohibited were only books, it appears that this Order hitherto is far insufficient to the end which it intends. Do we not see, not once or oftener, but weekly, that continued court-libel against the Parliament and city, printed, as the wet sheets can witness, and dispersed among us for all that licensing can do? Yet this is the prime service, a man would think, wherein this Order should give proof of itself. *If it were executed*, you'll say. But certain, if execution be remiss or blindfold now and in this particular, what will it be hereafter and in other books? If then the Order shall not be vain and frustrate, behold a new labour, Lords and Commons: ye must repeal and proscribe all scandalous and unlicensed books already printed and divulged; after ye have drawn them up into a list, that all may know which are condemned, and which not; and ordain that no foreign books be delivered out of custody, till they have been read over. This office will require the whole time of not a few overseers,

8 *scanting:* limiting.　11 *frivolous:* manifestly futile.　29 *frustrate:* of no effect.　31 *divulged:* published.

and those no vulgar men. There be also books which are partly useful and excellent, partly culpable and pernicious; this work will ask as many more officials, to make expurgations and expunctions, that the commonwealth of learning be not damnified. In fine, when the multitude of books increase upon their hands, ye must be fain to catalogue all those printers who are found frequently offending, and forbid the importation of their whole suspected typography. In a word, that this your Order may be exact, and not deficient, ye must reform it perfectly according to the model of Trent and Seville, which I know ye abhor to do.

Yet though ye should condescend to this, which God forbid, the Order still would be but fruitless and defective to that end whereto ye meant it. If to prevent sects and schisms, who is so unread or so uncatechised in story, that hath not heard of many sects refusing books as a hindrance, and preserving their doctrine unmixed for many ages, only by unwritten traditions? The Christian faith, for that was once a schism, is not unknown to have spread all over Asia, ere any gospel or epistle was seen in writing. If the amendment of manners be aimed at, look into Italy and Spain, whether those places be one scruple the better, the honester, the wiser, the chaster, since all the inquisitional rigour that hath been executed upon books.

Another reason, whereby to make it plain that this Order will miss the end it seeks, consider by the quality which ought to be in every licenser. It cannot be denied but that he who is made judge to sit upon the birth or death of books, whether they may be wafted into this world or not, had need to be a man above the common measure both studious, learned, and judicious; there may be else no mean mistakes in the censure of what is passable or not; which is also no mean injury. If he be of such worth as behoves him, there cannot be a more tedious and unpleasing journey-work, a greater loss of time levied upon his

1 *vulgar:* unlearned. 4 *expunctions:* erasures. 10 *Trent:* the Council of Trent. *Seville:* the Spanish Inquisition. 15 *story:* history. 25 *by the quality:* in view of the qualifications. 33 *journey-work:* hackwork.

head, than to be made the perpetual reader of unchosen books and pamphlets, ofttimes huge volumes. There is no book that is acceptable unless at certain seasons; but to be enjoined the reading of that at all times, and in a hand scarce legible, whereof three pages would not down at any time in the fairest print, is an imposition which I cannot believe how he that values time and his own studies, or is but of a sensible nostril, should be able to endure. In this one thing I crave leave of the present licensers to be pardoned for so thinking; who doubtless took this office up looking on it through their obedience to the Parliament, whose command perhaps made all things seem easy and un-laborious to them; but that this short trial hath wearied them out already, their own expressions and excuses to them who make so many journeys to solicit their license are testimony enough. Seeing therefore those who now possess the employ-ment, by all evident signs, wish themselves well rid of it, and that no man of worth, none that is not a plain unthrift of his own hours, is ever likely to succeed them, except he mean to put himself to the salary of a press-corrector, we may easily foresee what kind of licensers we are to expect hereafter: either ignorant, imperious, and remiss, or basely pecuniary. This is what I had to show, wherein this Order cannot conduce to that end whereof it bears the intention.

I lastly proceed from the no good it can do, to the manifest hurt it causes, in being first the greatest discouragement and affront that can be offered to learning and to learned men.

It was the complaint and lamentation of prelates, upon every least breath of a motion to remove pluralities, and distribute more equally church revenues, that then all learning would be for ever dashed and discouraged. But as for that opinion, I never found cause to think that the tenth part of learning stood or fell with the clergy; nor could I ever but hold it for a sordid and unworthy speech of any churchman who had a competency left him. If therefore ye be loth to dishearten

5 *would not down:* could not be swallowed.   7 *sensible nostril:* sensitive palate.   28 *pluralities:* the holding of more than one benefice.   33 *it:* the expression of such an opinion.

utterly and discontent, not the mercenary crew of false pretenders to learning, but the free and ingenuous sort of such as evidently were born to study, and love learning for itself, not for lucre, or any other end, but the service of God and of truth, and perhaps that lasting fame and perpetuity of praise which God and good men have consented shall be the reward of those whose published labours advance the good of mankind — then know: that so far to distrust the judgment and the honesty of one who hath but a common repute in learning, and never yet offended, as not to count him fit to print his mind without a tutor and examiner, lest he should drop a schism, or something of corruption, is the greatest displeasure and indignity to a free and knowing spirit that can be put upon him.

What advantage is it to be a man over it is to be a boy at school, if we have only escaped the ferula to come under the fescue of an imprimatur? If serious and elaborate writings, as if they were no more than the theme of a grammar lad under his pedagogue, must not be uttered without the cursory eyes of a temporizing and extemporizing licenser? He who is not trusted with his own actions, his drift not being known to be evil, and standing to the hazard of law and penalty, has no great argument to think himself reputed in the commonwealth wherein he was born for other than a fool or a foreigner. When a man writes to the world, he summons up all his reason and deliberation to assist him; he searches, meditates, is industrious, and likely consults and confers with his judicious friends; after all which done, he takes himself to be informed in what he writes as well as any that writ before him. If, in this, the most consummate act of his fidelity and ripeness, no years, no industry, no former proof of his abilities can bring him to that state of maturity, as not to be still mistrusted and suspected, unless he carry all his considerate diligence, all his midnight watchings and expense of Palladian oil, to the hasty view of an unleisured

15 *ferula*: cane. 16 *fescue*: pointer used in teaching. *imprimatur*: permit (see page 22 line 26). 17 *theme*: essay. 18 *uttered*: published. *cursory*: surveying. 19 *temporizing*: timeserving. *extemporizing*: improvizing. 20 *drift*: aim. 21 *standing to*: being under. 33 *Palladian*: learned.

licenser, (perhaps much his younger, perhaps far his inferior in judgment, perhaps one who never knew the labour of book-writing), and — if he be not repulsed or slighted — must appear in print like a puny with his guardian, and his censor's hand on the back of his title to be his bail and surety that he is no idiot or seducer, it cannot be but a dishonour and derogation to the author, to the book, to the privilege and dignity of learning.

And what if the author shall be one so copious of fancy as to have many things, well worth the adding, come into his mind after licensing, while the book is yet under the press, (which not seldom happens to the best and diligentest writers); and that perhaps a dozen times in one book? The printer dares not go beyond his licensed copy; so often then must the author trudge to his leave-giver, that those his new insertions may be viewed; and many a jaunt will be made ere that licenser — for it must be the same man — can either be found, or found at leisure. Meanwhile, either the press must stand still, which is no small damage, or the author lose his accuratest thoughts and send the book forth worse than he had made it, which to a diligent writer is the greatest melancholy and vexation that can befall.

And how can a man teach with authority, which is the life of teaching, how can he be a doctor in his book, as he ought to be or else had better be silent, whenas all he teaches, all he delivers, is but under the tuition, under the correction, of his pat-riarchal licenser to blot or alter what precisely accords not with the hide-bound humour which he calls his judgment? When every acute reader, upon the first sight of a pedantic licence, will be ready with these like words to ding the book a quoit's distance from him: 'I hate a pupil teacher; I endure not an instructor that comes to me under the wardship of an overseeing fist. I know nothing of the licenser, but that I have his own hand here for his arrogance; who shall warrant me his

4 *puny:* backward boy. 5 *hand:* writing. 11 *under:* in. 20 *had:* would have. 28 *humour:* mentality. 29 *pedantic:* schoolmasterish. 30 *ding:* fling.

judgment?' 'The State, sir,' replies the stationer; but has a
quick return: 'The State shall be my governors, but not my
critics; they may be mistaken in the choice of a licenser, as
easily as this licenser may be mistaken in an author: this is
some common stuff'; and he might add from Sir Francis
Bacon that 'such authorized books are but the language of the
times.' For though a licenser should happen to be judicious
more than ordinary, which will be a great jeopardy of the next
succession, yet his very office and his commission enjoins him
to let pass nothing but what is vulgarly received already.

Nay, which is more lamentable, if the work of any deceased
author, though never so famous in his lifetime, and even to this
day, come to their hands for licence to be printed or reprinted,
if there be found in his book one sentence of a venturous edge,
uttered in the height of zeal — and who knows whether it
might not be the dictate of a divine spirit? — yet, not suiting with
every low decrepit humour of their own, though it were Knox
himself, the reformer of a kingdom, that spake it, they will not
pardon him their dash; the sense of that great man shall to all
posterity be lost, for the fearfulness, or the presumptuous
rashness of a perfunctory licenser. And to what an author this
violence hath been lately done, and in what book of greatest
consequence to be faithfully published, I could now instance,
but shall forbear till a more convenient season.

Yet if these things be not resented seriously and timely by
them who have the remedy in their power, but that such iron
moulds as these shall have authority to gnaw out the choicest
periods of exquisitest books, and to commit such a treacherous
fraud against the orphan remainders of worthiest men after
death, the more sorrow will belong to that hapless race of men,
whose misfortune it is to have understanding. Henceforth let
no man care to learn, or care to be more than worldly wise: for
certainly in higher matters to be ignorant and slothful, to be a

1 *stationer:* publisher and bookseller. 2 *return:* retort. 8–9 *be a great
jeopardy . . . succession:* put his successor in a tricky position 10 *vulgarly:* generally. 19 *dash:* erasure. 26 *iron moulds:* rusts. 28 *periods:*
sentences.

common steadfast dunce, will be the only pleasant life, and only in request.

And as it is a particular disesteem of every knowing person alive, and most injurious to the written labours and monuments of the dead, so to me it seems an undervaluing and vilifying of the whole nation. I cannot set so lightly by all the invention, the art, the wit, the grave and solid judgment which is in England, as that it can be comprehended in any twenty capacities how good soever; much less that it should not pass except their superintendence be over it, except it be sifted and strained with their strainers, that it should be uncurrent without their manual stamp. Truth and understanding are not such wares as to be monopolized and traded in by tickets, and statutes, and standards. We must not think to make a staple commodity of all the knowledge in the land, to mark and license it like our broadcloth and our woolpacks. What is it but a servitude like that imposed by the Philistines, not to be allowed the sharpening of our own axes and coulters, but we must repair from all quarters to twenty licensing forges? Had anyone written and divulged erroneous things and scandalous to honest life, misusing and forfeiting the esteem had of his reason among men: if, after conviction, this only censure were adjudged him, that he should never henceforth write but what were first examined by an appointed officer, whose hand should be annexed to pass his credit for him that now he might be safely read, it could not be apprehended less than a disgraceful punishment. Whence to include the whole nation, and those that never yet thus offended, under such a diffident and suspectful prohibition, may plainly be understood what a disparagement it is. So much the more, whenas debtors and delinquents may walk abroad without a keeper, but unoffensive books must not stir forth without a visible jailor in their title.

Nor is it to the common people less than a reproach; for if

6 *set so lightly by:* value so little. 13 *tickets:* certificates of trading prerogatives. 14 *statutes:* controlling trade. *standards:* of measurement. *staple:* chartered. 28 *diffident:* mistrustful.

we so jealous over them, as that we dare not trust them with an
English pamphlet, what do we but censure them for a giddy,
vicious, and ungrounded people: in such a sick and weak
estate of faith and discretion, as to be able to take nothing
down but through the pipe of a licenser? That this is care or love
of them, we cannot pretend, whenas in those popish places
where the laity are most hated and despised the same strictness
is used over them. Wisdom we cannot call it, because it stops
but one breach of license, nor that neither: whenas those cor-
ruptions, which it seeks to prevent, break in faster at other
doors which cannot be shut.

And in conclusion it reflects to the disrepute of our ministers
also, of whose labours we should hope better, and of the
proficiency which their flock reaps by them, than that after all
this light of the gospel which is, and is to be, and all this
continual preaching, they should be still frequented with such
an unprincipled, unedified and laic rabble, as that the whiff of
every new pamphlet should stagger them out of their catechism
and Christian walking. This may have much reason to dis-
courage the ministers when such a low conceit is had of all
their exhortations, and the benefiting of their hearers, as that
they are not thought fit to be turned loose to three sheets of
paper without a licenser; that all the sermons, all the lectures
preached, printed, vented in such numbers and such volumes
as have now well-nigh made all other books unsaleable, should
not be armour enough against one single enchiridion, without
the castle St. Angelo of an Imprimatur.

And lest some should persuade ye, Lords and Commons,
that these arguments of learned men's discouragement at this
your order are mere flourishes and not real, I could recount
what I have seen and heard in other countries, where this kind
of inquisition tyrannises; when I have sat among their learned
men, for that honour I had, and been counted happy to be

5 *the pipe:* the tube used to feed very weak patients.   16 *frequented
with:* attended by.   17 *laic:* lay.   18 *them:* the 'laic rabble'.
20 *conceit:* opinion.   22 *they:* their hearers.   24 *vented:* sold.   26 *enchiridion:* i. handbook *and* ii. dagger.   27 *castle St. Angelo ... Imprimatur:* the protection of a papal licence.

born in such a place of philosophic freedom as they supposed
England was, while themselves did nothing but bemoan the
servile condition into which learning amongst them was
brought: that this was it which had damped the glory of Italian
wits, that nothing had been there written now these many
years but flattery and fustian. There it was that I found and
visited the famous Galileo grown old, a prisoner to the
Inquisition, for thinking in astronomy otherwise than the
Franciscan and Dominican licencers thought.

And though I knew that England then was groaning loudest
under the prelatical yoke, nevertheless I took it as a pledge of
future happiness, that other nations were so persuaded of her
liberty. Yet was it beyond my hope that those worthies were
then breathing in her air, who should be her leaders to such a
deliverance as shall never be forgotten by any revolution of
time that this world hath to finish. When that was once begun,
it was as little in my fear that what words of complaint I heard
among learned men of other parts uttered against the Inquisition, the same I should hear by as learned men at home uttered
in time of Parliament against an order of licensing: and that so
generally that, when I had disclosed myself a companion of
their discontent, I might say, (if without envy), that he whom
an honest quaestorship had endeared to the Sicilians was not
more by them importuned against Verres, than the favourable
opinion which I had among many who honour ye, and are
known and respected by ye, loaded me with entreaties and
persuasions, that I would not despair to lay together that
which just reason should bring into my mind, toward the
removal of an undeserved thraldom upon learning. That this is
not therefore the disburdening of a particular fancy, but the
common grievance of all those who had prepared their minds
and studies above the vulgar pitch to advance truth in others,
and from others to entertain it, thus much may satisfy.

And in their name I shall for neither friend nor foe conceal
what the general murmur is: that if it come to inquisitioning
again and licensing, and that we are so timorous of ourselves,
6 *fustian:* bombast. 22 *envy:* causing jealousy. 33 *entertain:* receive.

and so suspicious of all men, as to fear each book, and the shaking of every leaf, before we know what the contents are; if some who but of late were little better than silenced from preaching, shall come now to silence us from reading except what they please, it cannot be guessed what is intended by some but a second tyranny over learning: and will soon put it out of controversy that bishops and presbyters are the same to us, both name and thing. That those evils of prelaty, which before from five or six and twenty sees were distributively charged upon the whole people, will now light wholly upon learning, is not obscure to us: whenas now the pastor of a small unlearned parish on the sudden shall be exalted archbishop over a large diocese of books, and yet not remove, but keep his other cure too, a mystical pluralist. He who but of late cried down the sole ordination of every novice bachelor of art, and denied sole jurisdiction over the simplest parishioner, shall now, at home in his private chair, assume both these over worthiest and excellentest books and ablest authors that write them.

This is not — Ye Covenants and Protestations that we have made! — this is not to put down prelaty; this is but to chop an episcopacy; this is but to translate the palace metropolitan from one kind of dominion into another; this is but an old canonical sleight of commuting our penance. To startle thus betimes at a mere unlicensed pamphlet will after a while be afraid of every conventicle, and a while after will make a conventicle of every Christian meeting. But I am certain that a state governed by the rules of justice and fortitude, or a church built and founded upon a rock of faith and true knowledge, cannot be so pusillanimous. While things are yet not constituted in religion, that freedom of writing should be restrained by a discipline imitated from the prelates, and learnt by them from the Inquisition, to shut us up all again into the breast of a licencer,

7 *out of:* beyond. 8 *name and thing:* in name and in reality. 14 *mystical:* mysterious. *He:* the zealous anti-prelatist. *cried down:* declared illegal. 21 *chop:* barter. 22 *the palace metropolitan:* Lambeth Palace. 23 *canonical sleight:* trick of canon law. 24 *commuting ... penance:* buying indulgences. 26 *conventicle:* Presbyterian meeting.

must needs give cause of doubt and discouragement to all
learned and religious men.

Who cannot but discern the fineness of this politic drift, and
who are the contrivers: that while bishops were to be baited
down, then all presses might be open; it was the people's
birthright and privilege in time of Parliament, it was the
breaking forth of light? But now, the bishops abrogated and
voided out of the Church, as if our Reformation sought no
more but to make room for others into their seats under another
name, the episcopal arts begin to bud again; the cruse of truth
must run no more oil; liberty of printing must be enthralled
again under a prelatical commission of twenty; the privilege of
the people nullified; and, which is worse, the freedom of
learning must groan again and to her old fetters: all this the
Parliament yet sitting! Although their own late arguments and
defences against the prelates might remember them that this
obstructing violence meets, for the most part, with an event
utterly opposite to the end which it drives at: instead of suppressing sects and schisms, it raises them and invests them with
a reputation. 'The punishing of wits enhances their authority,'
saith the Viscount St. Albans; 'and a forbidden writing is
thought to be a certain spark of truth that flies up in the faces of
them who seek to tread it out.' This order, therefore, may prove
a nursing mother to sects, but I shall easily show how it will be
a stepdame to truth: and first by disenabling us to the maintenance of what is known already.

Well knows he who uses to consider, that our faith and knowledge thrives by exercise, as well as our limbs and complexion.
Truth is compared in scripture to a streaming fountain; if her
waters flow not in a perpetual progression, they sicken into a
muddy pool of conformity and tradition. A man may be a
heretic in the truth; and if he believe things only because his
pastor says so, or the Assembly so determines, without

4 *baited down:* chained, like baited bears.   7 *abrogated:* done away
with.   8 *voided:* ejected.   16 *remember:* remind.   21 *Viscount St.
Albans:* Sir Francis Bacon.   28 *complexion:* constitution.   32 *in:*
though he believe in.   33 *Assembly:* supreme ecclesiastical court of
the Presbyterians.

knowing other reason, though his belief be true, yet the very truth he holds becomes his heresy.

There is not any burden that some would gladlier post off to another than the charge and care of their religion. There be — who knows not that there be? — of protestants and professors who live and die in as arrant an implicit faith as any lay papist of Loretto. A wealthy man, addicted to his pleasure and to his profits, finds religion to be a traffic so entangled, and of so many piddling accounts, that of all mysteries he cannot skill to keep a stock going upon that trade. What should he do? Fain he would have the name to be religious, fain he would bear up with his neighbours in that. What does he, therefore, but resolves to give over toiling, and to find himself out some factor, to whose care and credit he may commit the whole managing of his religious affairs? Some divine of note and estimation that must be. To him he adheres, resigns the whole warehouse of his religion, with all the locks and keys, into his custody; and indeed makes the very person of that man his religion; esteems his associating with him a sufficient evidence and commendatory of his own piety. So that a man may say his religion is now no more within himself, but is become a dividual movable, and goes and comes near him, according as that good man frequents the house. He entertains him, gives him gifts, feasts him, lodges him; his religion comes home at night, prays, is liberally supped, and sumptuously laid to sleep; rises, is saluted, and after the malmsey, or some well-spiced brewage, and better breakfasted than He whose morning appetite would have gladly fed on green figs between Bethany and Jerusalem, his religion walks abroad at eight, and leaves his kind entertainer in the shop trading all day without his religion.

Another sort there be who, when they hear that all things shall be ordered, all things regulated and settled, nothing written but what passes through the custom-house of certain

5 *professors:* Puritans. 9 *mysteries:* crafts. *skill:* manage. 11 *bear up:* keep abreast of. 20 *commendatory:* commendation. 22 *dividual movable:* something separable and removable.

publicans that have the tunnaging and the poundaging of all
free-spoken truth, will straight give themselves up into your
hands, make 'em and cut 'em out what religion ye please.
There be delights, there be recreations and jolly pastimes
that will fetch the day about from sun to sun, and rock the
tedious year as in a delightful dream. What need they torture
their heads with that which others have taken so strictly
and so unalterably into their own purveying? These are the
fruits which a dull ease and cessation of our knowledge will
bring forth among the people. How goodly and how to be
wished were such an obedient unanimity as this! What a
fine conformity would it starch us all into! Doubtless a staunch
and solid piece of framework as any January could freeze
together.

Nor much better will be the consequence even among the
clergy themselves. It is no new thing never heard of before for
a parochial minister, who has his reward and is at his Hercules'
pillars in a warm benefice, to be easily inclinable, if he have
nothing else that may rouse up his studies, to finish his circuit
in an English Concordance and a topic folio, the gatherings and
savings of a sober graduateship, a Harmony and a Catena;
treading the constant round of certain common doctrinal heads,
attended with the uses, motives, marks and means, out of which,
(as out of an alphabet or sol-fa), by forming and transforming,
joining and disjoining variously, a little bookcraft and two
hours' meditation might furnish him unspeakably to the performance of more than a weekly charge of sermoning — not to
reckon up the infinite helps of interlinearies, breviaries,
synopses, and other loitering gear! But as for the multitude of
sermons ready printed and piled up, on every text that is not

---

1 *publicans:* tax-collectors. *the tunnaging and the poundaging of:* the
customs duties on. 17–18 *parochial:* i. of a parish *and* ii. narrow-
minded. *is at his Hercules' pillars:* has reached his goal. 20 *topic
folio:* commonplace book. 21 *Harmony:* synopsis of the four gospels, in which apparently incongruous accounts are 'harmonized'.
Catena: list of authorities forming a Bible-commentary. 24 *sol-fa:*
musical scale. 28 *interlinearies:* interlined translations. *breviaries:*
abridgements. 29 *synopses:* outlines. *loitering:* lazy.

difficult, our London trading St. Thomas in his vestry, and add
to boot St. Martin and St. Hugh, have not within their hal-
lowed limits more vendible ware of all sorts ready made: so
that penury he never need fear of pulpit provision, having
where so plenteously to refresh his magazine. But if his rear
and flanks be not impaled, if his back door be not secured by
the rigid licenser, but that a bold book may now and then issue
forth and give the assault to some of his old collections in their
trenches, it will concern him then to keep waking, to stand in
watch, to set good guards and sentinels about his received
opinions, to walk the round and counter-round with his fellow
inspectors, fearing lest any of his flock be seduced, who also
then would be better instructed, better exercised and disciplined. And God send that the fear of this diligence, which
must then be used, do not make us affect the laziness of a
licensing church.

For if we be sure we are in the right, and do not hold the
truth guiltily, which becomes not, if we ourselves condemn not
our own weak and frivolous teaching, and the people for an
untaught and irreligious gadding rout, what can be more fair
than when a man judicious, learned, and of a conscience, for
aught we know, as good as theirs that taught us what we know,
shall not privily from house to house, which is more dangerous,
but openly by writing publish to the world what his opinion is,
what his reasons, and wherefore that which is now thought
cannot be sound? Christ urged it as wherewith to justify himself, that he preached in public; yet writing is more public than
preaching; and more easy to refutation, if need be, there being
so many whose business and profession merely it is to be the
champions of truth; which if they neglect, what can be im-
puted but their sloth, or inability?

Thus much we are hindered and disinured by this course
of licensing towards the true knowledge of what we seem to

1-2 *St. Thomas . . . St. Martin and St. Hugh:* shopping-centres in
London, with names like those of churches. 6 *impaled:* palisaded.
9 *concern:* be necessary for. 18 *guiltily:* feebly. 30 *what can be:* to
what can it be.

E

know. For how much it hurts and hinders the licensers themselves in the calling of their ministry, more than any secular employment, if they will discharge that office as they ought, so that of necessity they must neglect either the one duty or the other, I insist not, because it is a particular, but leave it to their own conscience how they will decide it there.

There is yet behind of what I purposed to lay open: the incredible loss and detriment that this plot of licensing puts us to. More than if some enemy at sea should stop up all our havens and ports and creeks, it hinders and retards the importation of our richest merchandise, truth; nay, it was first established and put in practice by antichristian malice and mystery on set purpose to extinguish, if it were possible, the light of Reformation, and to settle falsehood; little differing from that policy wherewith the Turk upholds his Alcoran by the prohibition of printing. 'Tis not denied, but gladly confessed, we are to send our thanks and vows to heaven, louder than most of nations, for that great measure of truth which we enjoy, especially in those main points between us and the pope with his appurtenances the prelates; but he who thinks we are to pitch our tent here, and have attained the utmost prospect of Reformation that the mortal glass wherein we contemplate can show us, till we come to beatific vision, that man by this very opinion declares that he is yet far short of truth.

Truth indeed came once into the world with her divine Master, and was a perfect shape most glorious to look on: but when he ascended, and his apostles after him were laid asleep, then straight arose a wicked race of deceivers, who, as that story goes of the Egyptian Typhon with his conspirators, how they dealt with the good Osiris, took the virgin Truth, hewed her lovely form into a thousand pieces, and scattered them to the four winds. From that time ever since, the sad friends of Truth, such as durst appear, imitating the careful search that Isis made for the mangled body of Osiris, went up and down gathering up limb by limb still as they could find them. We

12 *antichristian:* Roman Catholic. *mystery:* fraud. 23 *beatific vision:* the vision of God face to face.

have not yet found them all, Lords and Commons, nor ever shall do, till her Master's second coming; he shall bring together every joint and member, and shall mould them into an immortal feature of loveliness and perfection. Suffer not these licensing prohibitions to stand at every place of opportunity forbidding and disturbing them that continue seeking, that continue to do our obsequies to the torn body of our martyred saint.

We boast our light; but if we look not wisely on the sun itself, it smites us into darkness. Who can discern those planets that are oft combust, and those stars of brightest magnitude that rise and set with the sun, until the opposite motion of their orbs bring them to such a place in the firmament, where they may be seen evening or morning? The light which we have gained was given us, not to be ever staring on, but by it to discover onward things more remote from our knowledge. It is not the unfrocking of a priest, the unmitring of a bishop, and the removing him from off the Presbyterian shoulders that will make us a happy nation; no, if other things as great in the Church, and in the rule of life both economical and political, be not looked into and reformed, we have looked so long upon the blaze that Zuinglius and Calvin hath beaconed up to us, that we are stark blind. There be who perpetually complain of schisms and sects, and make it such a calamity that any man dissents from their maxims. 'Tis their own pride and ignorance which causes the disturbing, who neither will hear with meekness nor can convince; yet all must be suppressed which is not found in their Syntagma. They are the troublers, they are the dividers of unity, who neglect and permit not others to unite those dissevered pieces which are yet wanting to the body of Truth. To be still searching what we know not by what we know, still closing up truth to truth as we find it (for all her body is homogeneal and proportional), this is the golden rule

4 *feature:* shape.   10 *smites us into darkness:* blinds us.   11 *combust:* within 8° 30′ of the sun.   20 *economical:* domestic.   22 *beaconed up:* lighted up as a beacon.   28 *Syntagma:* handbook.   31 *searching:* exploring.   33 *homogeneal:* in relation.

in theology as well as in arithmetic, and makes up the best harmony in a church, not the forced and outward union of cold and neutral and inwardly divided minds.

Lords and Commons of England, consider what nation it is whereof ye are and whereof ye are the governors: a nation not slow and dull, but of a quick, ingenious, and piercing spirit; acute to invent, subtle and sinewy to discourse, not beneath the reach of any point the highest that human capacity can soar to. Therefore the studies of learning in her deepest sciences have been so ancient and so eminent among us, that writers of good antiquity and ablest judgement have been persuaded that even the school of Pythagoras and the Persian wisdom took beginning from the old philosophy of this island. And that wise and civil Roman, Julius Agricola, who governed once here for Caesar, preferred the natural wits of Britain before the laboured studies of the French. Nor is it for nothing that the grave and frugal Transylvanian sends out yearly from as far as the mountainous borders of Russia and beyond the Hercynian wilderness, not their youth, but their staid men, to learn our language and our theological arts.

Yet that which is above all this, the favour and the love of heaven, we have great argument to think in a peculiar manner propitious and propending towards us. Why else was this nation chosen before any other, that out of her, as out of Sion, should be proclaimed and sounded forth the first tidings and trumpet of Reformation to all Europe? And had it not been the obstinate perverseness of our prelates against the divine and admirable spirit of Wycliffe, to suppress him as a schismatic and innovator, perhaps neither the Bohemian Hus and Jerome, no, nor the name of Luther or of Calvin had been ever known: the glory of reforming all our neighbours had been completely ours. But now, as our obdurate clergy have with violence demeaned the matter, we are become hitherto the latest and the backwardest scholars, of whom God offered to have made us the teachers. Now once again by all concurrence of signs, and by the general instinct of holy and devout men, as

23 *propending*: inclining towards. 33 *demeaned*: conducted.

they daily and solemnly express their thoughts, God is decreeing to begin some new and great period in his Church, even to the reforming of Reformation itself. What does he then but reveal himself to his servants, and, as his manner is, first to his Englishmen? I say, as his manner is, first to us: though we mark not the method of his counsels, and are unworthy.

Behold now this vast city: a city of refuge, the mansion house of liberty, encompassed and surrounded with his protection; the shop of war hath not there more anvils and hammers waking, to fashion out the plates and instruments of armed Justice in defence of beleaguered Truth, than there be pens and heads there, sitting by their studious lamps, musing, searching, revolving new notions and ideas wherewith to present, as with their homage and their fealty, the approaching Reformation: others as fast reading, trying all things, assenting to the force of reason and convincement. What could a man require more from a nation so pliant and so prone to seek after knowledge? What wants there to such a towardly and pregnant soil but wise and faithful labourers, to make a knowing people, a nation of prophets, of sages, and of worthies? We reckon more than five months yet to harvest; there need not be five weeks: had we but eyes to lift up, the fields are white already!

Where there is much desire to learn, there of necessity will be much arguing, much writing, many opinions; for opinion in good men is but knowledge in the making. Under these fantastic terrors of sect and schism, we wrong the earnest and zealous thirst after knowledge and understanding which God hath stirred up in this city. What some lament of, we rather should rejoice at, should rather praise this pious forwardness among men to reassume the ill-reputed care of their religion into their own hands again. A little generous prudence, a little forbearance of one another, and some grain of charity might win all these diligences to join and unite in one general and brotherly search after truth, could we but forego this prelatical tradition of crowding free consciences and Christian liberties into canons

18 *towardly:* tractable. 27 *fantastic:* fanciful.

and precepts of men. I doubt not, if some great and worthy stranger should come among us, wise to discern the mould and temper of a people and how to govern it, observing the high hopes and aims, the diligent alacrity of our extended thoughts and reasonings in the pursuance of truth and freedom, but that he would cry out as Pyrrhus did, admiring the Roman docility and courage: 'If such were my Epirots, I would not despair the greatest design that could be attempted to make a church or kingdom happy.'

Yet these are the men cried out against for schismatics and sectaries; as if, while the temple of the Lord was building, some cutting, some squaring the marble, others hewing the cedars, there should be a sort of irrational men, who could not consider there must be many schisms and many dissections made in the quarry and in the timber, ere the house of God can be built. And when every stone is laid artfully together, it cannot be united into a continuity, it can but be contiguous in this world; neither can every piece of the building be of one form; nay, rather the perfection consists in this: that out of many moderate varieties and brotherly dissimilitudes that are not vastly disproportional, arises the goodly and the graceful symmetry that commends the whole pile and structure.

Let us therefore be more considerate builders, more wise in spiritual architecture, when great reformation is expected. For now the time seems come, wherein Moses, the great prophet, may sit in heaven rejoicing to see that memorable and glorious wish of his fulfilled, when not only our seventy elders but all the Lord's people are becoming prophets. No marvel then though some men, and some good men too perhaps, but young in goodness, as Joshua then was, envy them. They fret, and out of their own weakness are in agony, lest those divisions and subdivisions will undo us. The adversary again applauds, and waits the hour: when they have branched themselves out, saith he, small enough into parties and partitions, then will be our time. Fool! he sees not the firm root, out of which we all grow, though into branches; nor will beware until he see our

7 *Epirots:* men of Epirus. 17 *contiguous:* touching, but separate.

small divided maniples cutting through at every angle of his ill-united and unwieldy brigade. And that we are to hope better of all these supposed sects and schisms, and that we shall not need that solicitude (honest perhaps, though over-timorous) of them that vex in this behalf, but shall laugh in the end at those malicious applauders of our differences, I have these reasons to persuade me.

First, when a city shall be as it were besieged and blocked about, her navigable river infested, inroads and incursions round, defiance and battle oft rumoured to be marching up even to her walls and suburb trenches, that then the people, or the greater part, more than at other times, wholly taken up with the study of highest and most important matters to be reformed, should be disputing, reasoning, reading, inventing, discoursing, even to a rarity and admiration, things not before discoursed or written of, argues first a singular goodwill, contentedness and confidence in your prudent foresight and safe government, Lords and Commons; and from thence derives itself to a gallant bravery and well grounded contempt of their enemies, as if there were no small number of as great spirits among us, as his was, who when Rome was nigh besieged by Hannibal, being in the city, bought that piece of ground at no cheap rate, whereon Hannibal himself encamped his own regiment.

Next, it is a lively and cheerful presage of our happy success and victory. For as in a body, when the blood is fresh, the spirits pure and vigorous not only to vital but to rational faculties, and those in the acutest and the pertest operations of wit and subtlety, it argues in what good plight and constitution the body is; so when the cheerfulness of the people is so sprightly up, as that it has not only wherewith to guard well its own freedom and safety but to spare, and to bestow upon the solidest and sublimest points of controversy and new invention, it betokens us not degenerated, nor drooping to a fatal decay, but casting off the old and wrinkled skin of corruption to outlive

1 *maniples:* companies of soldiers.   15 *admiration:* astonishment.
27 *vital:* physical.   28 *pertest:* most nimble.

these pangs and wax young again, entering the glorious ways of truth and prosperous virtue, destined to become great and honourable in these latter ages. Methinks I see in my mind a noble and puissant nation rousing herself like a strong man after sleep, and shaking her invincible locks. Methinks I see her as an eagle mewing her mighty youth, and kindling her un-dazzled eyes at the full midday beam; purging and unscaling her long-abused sight at the fountain itself of heavenly radiance; while the whole noise of timorous and flocking birds, with those also that love the twilight, flutter about, amazed at what she means, and in their envious gabble would prognosticate a year of sects and schisms.

What should ye do then? Should ye suppress all this flowery crop of knowledge and new light sprung up and yet springing daily in this city? Should ye set an oligarchy of twenty en-grossers over it, to bring a famine upon our minds again, when we shall know nothing but what is measured to us by their bushel? Believe it, Lords and Commons, they who counsel ye to such a suppressing do as good as bid ye suppress yourselves; and I will soon show how. If it be desired to know the im-mediate cause of all this free writing and free speaking, there cannot be assigned a truer than your own mild and free and humane government. It is the liberty, Lords and Commons, which your own valorous and happy counsels have purchased us, liberty which is the nurse of all great wits; this is that which hath rarefied and enlightened our spirits like the influence of heaven; this is that which hath enfranchised, enlarged and lifted up our apprehensions degrees above themselves.

Ye cannot make us now less capable, less knowing, less eagerly pursuing of the truth, unless ye first make yourselves, that made us so, less the lovers, less the founders of our true liberty. We can grow ignorant again, brutish, formal, and slavish, as ye found us; but you then must first become that

---

6 *mewing:* renewing. 11 *in their envious . . . prognosticate:* intend their envious squawkings to make the augurs predict. 15 *engrossers:* merchants who buy up large stocks and become monopolists. 27 *en-franchised:* unbound. *enlarged:* set free.

which ye cannot be, oppressive, arbitrary, and tyrannous, as
they were from whom ye have freed us. That our hearts are
now more capacious, our thoughts more erected to the search
and expectation of greatest and exactest things, is the issue of
your own virtue propagated in us; ye cannot suppress that,
unless ye reinforce an abrogated and merciless law that
fathers may despatch at will their own children. And who shall
then stick closest to ye, and excite others? Not he who takes up
arms for coat and conduct, and his four nobles of Danegeld.
Although I dispraise not the defence of just immunities, yet
love my peace better, if that were all. Give me the liberty to
know, to utter, and to argue freely according to conscience,
above all liberties.

What would be best advised, then, if it be found so hurtful
and so unequal to suppress opinions for the newness or the
unsuitableness to a customary acceptance, will not be my task
to say; I only shall repeat what I have learned from one of your
own honourable number, a right noble and pious lord, who,
had he not sacrificed his life and fortunes to the Church and
Commonwealth, we had not now missed and bewailed a worthy
and undoubted patron of this argument. Ye know him, I am
sure; yet I for honour's sake, and may it be eternal to him, shall
name him — the Lord Brook. He writing of episcopacy, and
by the way treating of sects and schisms, left ye his vote, or
rather now the last words of his dying charge, which I know
will ever be of dear and honoured regard with ye, so full of
meekness and breathing charity, that, next to His last testament
who bequeathed love and peace to his disciples, I cannot call to
mind where I have read or heard words more mild and peaceful.
He there exhorts us to hear with patience and humility those,
however they be miscalled, that desire to live purely, in such a
use of God's ordinances as the best guidance of their conscience
gives them, and to tolerate them, though in some disconformity
to ourselves. The book itself will tell us more at large, being

9 *for coat and conduct:* against taxation to clothe and maintain troops.
Danegeld: ship-money.   11 *if that were all:* if nothing but immunity
from taxes were at stake.   15 *unequal:* unjust.

published to the world and dedicated to the Parliament by him who, both for his life and for his death, deserves that what advice he left be not laid by without perusal.

And now the time in special is, by privilege to write and speak what may help to the further discussing of matters in agitation. The temple of Janus with his two controversal faces might now not unsignificantly be set open. And though all the winds of doctrine were let loose to play upon the earth, so Truth be in the field, we do injuriously by licensing and prohibiting to misdoubt her strength. Let her and Falsehood grapple; who ever knew Truth put to the worse in a free and open encounter? Her confuting is the best and surest suppressing. He who hears what praying there is for light and clearer knowledge to be sent down among us, would think of other matters to be constituted beyond the discipline of Geneva, framed and fabricked already to our hands. Yet when the new light which we beg for shines in upon us, there be who envy and oppose, if it come not first in at their casements. What a collusion is this, whenas we are exhorted by the wise man to use diligence, to seek for wisdom as for hidden treasures early and late, that another order shall enjoin us to know nothing but by statute? When a man hath been labouring the hardest labour in the deep mines of knowledge; hath furnished out his findings in all their equipage; drawn forth his reasons as it were a battle ranged; scattered and defeated all objections in his way; calls out his adversary into the plain, offers him the advantage of wind and sun, if he please only that he may try the matter by dint of argument: for his opponents then to skulk, to lay ambushments, to keep a narrow bridge of licensing where the challenger should pass, though it be valour enough in soldiership, is but weakness and cowardice in the wars of Truth.

For who knows not that Truth is strong next to the Almighty?

6 *controversal:* looking in opposite directions.   12 *Her confuting:* confutation by her.   15 *the discipline of Geneva:* Presbyterianism. 19 *the wise man:* Solomon.   24 *equipage:* equipment.   25 *a battle:* an army.

She needs no policies, nor stratagems, nor licensings to make her victorious; those are the shifts and the defences that error uses against her power. Give her but room, and do not bind her when she sleeps, for then she speaks not true, as the old Proteus did, who spake oracles only when he was caught and bound; but then rather she turns herself into all shapes, except her own, and perhaps tunes her voice according to the time, as Micaiah did before Ahab, until she be adjured into her own likeness. Yet it is not impossible that she may have more shapes than one. What else is all that rank of things indifferent, wherein Truth may be on this side or on the other, without being unlike herself? What but a vain shadow else is the abolition of those ordinances, that handwriting nailed to the cross? What great purchase is this Christian liberty which Paul so often boasts of? His doctrine is, that he who eats or eats not, regards a day or regards it not, may do either to the Lord. How many other things might be tolerated in peace, and left to conscience, had we but charity, and were it not the chief stronghold of our hypocrisy to be ever judging one another!

I fear yet this iron yoke of outward conformity hath left a slavish print upon our necks; the ghost of a linen decency yet haunts us. We stumble and are impatient at the least dividing of one visible congregation from another, though it be not in fundamentals; and though our forwardness to suppress, and our backwardness to recover any enthralled piece of truth out of the gripe of custom, we care not to keep truth separated from truth, which is the fiercest rent and disunion of all. We do not see that, while we still affect by all means a rigid external formality, we may as soon fall again into a gross conforming stupidity, a stark and dead congealment of wood and hay and stubble forced and frozen together, which is more to the sudden degenerating of a church than many subdichotomies of petty schisms.

Not that I can think well of every light separation, or that all in a church is to be expected gold and silver and precious

21 *linen decency:* superficial decorum of surplices.   26 *care not to keep:* do not mind keeping.   32 *subdichotomies:* subdivisions.

stones; it is not possible for man to sever the wheat from the tares, the good fish from the other fry; that must be the angels' ministry at the end of mortal things. Yet if all cannot be of one mind (as who looks they should be?) this doubtless is more wholesome, more prudent, and more Christian: that many be tolerated rather than all compelled. I mean not tolerated popery and open superstition, which as it extirpates all religions and civil supremacies, so itself should be extirpate, provided first that all charitable and compassionate means be used to win and regain the weak and misled — that also which is impious or evil absolutely either against faith or manner no law can possibly permit, that intends not to unlaw itself — but those neighbouring differences, or rather indifferences, are what I speak of, whether in some point of doctrine or of discipline, which though they may be many, yet need not interrupt the unity of Spirit, if we could but find among us the bond of peace.

In the meanwhile if any one would write, and bring his helpful hand to the slow-moving Reformation which we labour under, if Truth have spoken to him before others, or but seemed at least to speak, who hath so bejesuited us that we should trouble that man with asking license to do so worthy a deed? And not consider this, that if it come to prohibiting, there is not aught more likely to be prohibited than truth itself; whose first appearance to our eyes, bleared and dimmed with prejudice and custom, is more unsightly and unplausible than many errors, even as the person is of many a great man slight and contemptible to see to. And what do they tell us vainly of new opinions, when this very opinion of theirs, that none must be heard but whom they like, is the worst and newest opinion of all others, and is the chief cause why sects and schisms do so much abound, and true knowledge is kept at distance from us? Besides yet a greater danger which is in it: for when God shakes a kingdom with strong and healthful commotions to a general reforming, 'tis not untrue that many sectaries and false teachers are then busiest in seducing; but yet more true it is, that God

28 *see to:* look at.

then raises to his own work men of rare abilities and more than common industry, not only to look back and revise what hath been taught heretofore, but to gain further and go on some new enlightened steps in the discovery of truth. For such is the order of God's enlightening his Church, to dispense and deal out by degrees his beam, so as our earthly eyes may best sustain it.

Neither is God appointed and confined, where and out of what place these his chosen shall be first heard to speak; for he sees not as man sees, chooses not as man chooses, lest we should devote ourselves again to set places, and assemblies, and outward callings of men; planting our faith one while in the old convocation house, and another while in the chapel at Westminster; when all the faith and religion that shall be there canonized is not sufficient, without plain convincement and the charity of patient instruction, to supple the least bruise of conscience, to edify the meanest Christian, who desires to walk in the Spirit, and not in the letter of human trust, for all the number of voices that can be there made; no, though Harry VII himself there, with all his liege tombs about him, should lend them voices from the dead, to swell their number.

And if the men be erroneous who appear to be the leading schismatics, what withholds us but our sloth, our self-will, and distrust in the right cause, that we do not give them gentle meetings and gentle dismissions, that we debate not and examine the matter thoroughly with liberal and frequent audience; if not for their sakes, yet for our own? Seeing no man who hath tasted learning, but will confess the many ways of profiting by those who, not contented with stale receipts, are able to manage and set forth new positions to the world. And were they but as the dust and cinders of our feet, so long as in that notion they may serve to polish and brighten the armoury of Truth, even for that respect they were not utterly to be cast away. But if they be of those whom God hath fitted for the

13 *convocation house:* Anglican assembly.   *chapel at Westminster:* Presbyterian assembly.   15 *canonized:* decreed by the Church. 20 *liege:* sovereign.   30 *manage:* take in hand.

special use of these times with eminent and ample gifts, and
those perhaps neither among the priests nor among the
pharisees, and we in the haste of a precipitant zeal shall make
no distinction, but resolve to stop their mouths, because we
fear they come with new and dangerous opinions, as we commonly forejudge them ere we understand them, no less than
woe to us, while, thinking thus to defend the gospel, we are
found the persecutors.

There have been not a few since the beginning of this
Parliament, both of the presbytery and others, who by their
unlicensed books to the contempt of an imprimatur first broke
that triple ice clung about our hearts, and taught the people to
see day: I hope that none of those were the persuaders to renew
upon us this bondage which they themselves have wrought so
much good by contemning. But if neither the check that Moses
gave to young Joshua, nor the countermand which our Saviour
gave to young John, who was so ready to prohibit those whom
he thought unlicensed, be not enough to admonish our elders
how unacceptable to God their testy mood of prohibiting is,
if neither their own remembrance what evil hath abounded in
the Church by this let of licensing, and what good they themselves have begun by transgressing it, be not enough, but that
they will persuade, and execute the most Dominican part of the
Inquisition over us, and are already with one foot in the stirrup
so active at suppressing, it would be no unequal distribution in
the first place to suppress the suppressors themselves: whom
the change of their condition hath puffed up more than their
late experience of harder times hath made wise.

And as for regulating the Press, let no man think to have the
honour of advising ye better than yourselves have done in that
Order published next before this: 'That no book be printed,
unless the printer's and the author's name, or at least the
printer's be registered.' Those which otherwise come forth, if
they be found mischievous and libellous, the fire and the
executioner will be the timeliest and the most effectual remedy

11 *to the:* in.   21 *let:* hindrance.   25 *unequal distribution:* injustice.
35 *the executioner*, whose duties included book-burning.

that man's prevention can use. For this authentic Spanish policy of licensing books, if I have said aught, will prove the most unlicensed book itself within a short while; and was the immediate image of a Star Chamber decree to that purpose made in those very times when that court did the rest of those her pious works, for which she is now fallen from the stars with Lucifer. Whereby ye may guess what kind of state prudence, what love of the people, what care of religion or good manners there was at the contriving, although with singular hypocrisy it pretended to bind books to their good behaviour. And how it got the upper hand of your precedent Order so well constituted before, if we may believe those men whose profession gives them cause to inquire most, it may be doubted there was in it the fraud of some old patentees and monopolizers in the trade of bookselling; who under pretence of the poor in their Company not to be defrauded, and the just retaining of each man his several copy, which God forbid should be gainsaid, brought divers glossing colours to the House, which were indeed but colours, and serving to no end except it be to exercise a superiority over their neighbours; men who do not therefore labour in an honest profession, to which learning is indebted, that they should be made other men's vassals. Another end is thought was aimed at by some of them in procuring by petition this Order, that, having power in their hands, malignant books might the easier scape abroad, as the event shows.

But of these sophisms and elenchs of merchandise I skill not. This I know, that errors in a good government and in a bad are equally almost incident; for what magistrate may not be misinformed, and much the sooner, if liberty of printing be reduced into the power of a few? But to redress willingly and speedily what hath been erred, and in highest authority to esteem a plain advertisement more than others have done a sumptuous

---

12 *those men:* the booksellers. 18 *glossing colours:* specious pretexts. 27 *sophisms:* fallacious arguments to establish false propositions. *elenchs:* fallacious arguments to refute true charges. *merchandise:* tradesmen. 29 *incident:* likely. 33 *advertisement:* warning.

bribe, is a virtue (honoured Lords and Commons) answerable to your highest actions, and whereof none can participate but greatest and wisest men.

1 *answerable to:* in harmony with.

Notes

p. 13, ll. 8–10. **And me perhaps . . . affected.** Milton had previously published anti-prelatical tracts, pamphlets on divorce and the treatise on education.

p. 13, l. 20. **trophy.** Success was not to be achieved until 1694: fifty years after the publication of *Areopagitica*, the press was freed.

p. 14, ll. 8–9. **If I now . . . do.** Milton's earlier praise of the Long Parliament is most enthusiastic in *An Apology for Smectymnuus* (1642).

p. 14, l. 9. **such a long obligement.** The Long Parliament met on the 3 November 1640, four years before *Areopagitica*.

p. 14, ll. 19–21. **rescuing the employment . . . encomium.** During the pamphlet-war about episcopacy, waged in London during 1641–2, Bishop Hall of Norwich was opposed by five Puritan ministers (led by Thomas Young, Milton's former tutor), whose initials formed the pen-name *Smectymnuus*. Milton defended them and attacked Bishop Hall.

'The sun', according to the bishop, 'looks not on a braver, nobler convocation than is that of King, Peers and Commons, whose equal justice and wise moderation shall eternally triumph. . . .'

Milton retorted that Bishop Hall, 'this private concoctor of malcontent . . . pretends to extol the Parliament . . . with . . . a suspicious and murmuring expression. . . . But I shall discover to ye, readers,' Milton continued in *An Apology for Smectymnuus*, with which he finally defeated Bishop Hall, 'that this his praising . . . is as full of nonsense and scholastic foppery as his meaning he himself discovers to be full of close malignity'.

p. 14, l. 31. **one of your published orders:** the Parliamentary Order of the 14 June 1643, forbidding the liberty of the Press.

p. 15, l. 5. **triennial parliament.** According to the Act passed in 1641, 'for the prevention of inconveniences happening by the long intermission of parliaments', Parliament should meet at least once in three years.

F

p. 15, ll. 5–6. **that jealous haughtiness . . . late:** Milton refers particularly to the Committee of Council, 'which,' according to Clarendon, 'was reproachfully after called "the Junto", and enviously then in the court "the cabinet".' Laud was the most influential member.

p. 15, ll. 18–19. **pride of a Hunnish . . . stateliness:** brutal aggressiveness of Huns and Vikings in the Dark Ages.

p. 15, ll. 21–3. **him who from his private house . . . established.** Isocrates (436–338 B.C.) wrote his *Areopagiticus* (355 B.C.) in the form of a speech in the *ecclesia*, or popular assembly, urging the restoration of a form of democracy in which the Areopagus had censorial powers (see Introduction, p. 4).

p. 15, l. 28. **Dion Prusaeus,** born at Prusa in Bithynia about A.D. 50, was a famous Greek rhetorician in the age of the Roman Emperors Nerva and Trajan. In his 'Rhodian Discourse', Dion protested against the custom at Rhodes of making old public statues, with altered inscriptions, serve new celebrities.

p. 15, l. 23. Milton, unlike Isocrates and Dion Prusaeus, lacks the stimulus of a warm, southern climate: but his genius is perhaps 'not the worst' in this chill, northern latitude. (Dr. Johnson, in his *Life of Milton*, ridicules the poet's fear 'lest the climate of his country might be too cold for flights of imagination'.)

p. 16, l. 16. **that order which . . . printing:** see Introduction, p. 2.

p. 16, ll. 20–1. **provides for the poor.** The Stationers Company seems to have used some of its profits charitably. The Parliamentary order implies this in its allusion to permits formerly 'granted to the said Company of Stationers for their reliefs and maintenance of their poor'.

p. 16, ll. 24–5. **quadragesimal and matrimonial.** Milton disliked the restrictions, not the exemptions from them. He thought that marriages should be (as they became by the Act of 1656) civil contracts, in no way sacramental.

p. 16, l. 25. **when the prelates expired.** Episcopacy was not formally abolished until 1646, but the bishops may be said to have 'expired' in 1642, when Charles gave his consent to the Bishops' Exclusion Bill.

p. 17, l. 15. dragon's teeth. Armed men sprang from dragon's teeth sown by Cadmus. Five of the men helped him to build Thebes.

p. 17, l. 33. All material things were thought by Aristotle and his followers to be ultimately composed of the four 'elements', earth, air, fire and water. The fifth element was believed to be spiritual.

p. 18, ll. 2–3. licence . . . licensing. Milton puns on the two words.

p. 18, l. 6. The **Inquisition** was instituted in 1231 as an ecclesiastical tribunal to discover and suppress heresy. Until Ferdinand and Isabella fostered it in Spain it was less active there than in Germany, France and Italy. In 1478 the first Grand Inquisitor, Torquemada, was appointed. He was a Spaniard, and the vigour of the 'Holy Office' was so great in Spain that the name 'Inquisition' came to mean 'Spanish Inquisition'. Milton uses it in that sense.

p. 18, ll. 7–8. Milton's criticism of the bishops is extended to some of the presbyters who are succeeding them.

p. 18, l. 13. judges of Areopagus: see Introduction, p. 5.

p. 18, l. 14. Protagoras (c. 480–c. 410 B.C.) was a sophist who taught in Athens. In 411, according to a later story, he was accused of impiety and his books were publicly burned. His offending theological treatise began: 'As to the gods, I cannot say whether they exist or not.'

p. 18, ll. 17–18. Vetus Comoedia: early Greek comedy, which abounded in personal satire. Aristophanes (444–c. 380 B.C.), its greatest exponent, ridiculed Euripides and Socrates unmercifully.

p. 18, ll. 19–21. as Cicero writes . . . showed: to stop both the reckless cleverness of other atheists (as Cicero writes) and the open road of libel, as the result showed.

The reference is to Cicero's *On the Nature of the Gods* I. 23; but Cicero says nothing about 'defaming'.

p. 18, l. 24. Epicurus (342–270 B.C.) taught in Athens that happiness, the highest good, can only be obtained by moderate living. His followers degraded his doctrine into a coarse philosophy of self-indulgence, and all Milton's references to him are hostile.

p. 18, ll. 24–5. that libertine school of Cyrene. The Cyrenaic

school of hedonist philosophy, which identified the chief
good with pleasure, was inspired by Aristippus and
flourished about 370 B.C. Aristippus was a native of Cyrene.
He came to Athens to be with Socrates, but returned home
after his friend's death.

p. 18, l. 25. **the Cynic impudence.** The scorn of the Cynic
philosophers was notorious. Believing that material and
social commitments make happiness impossible, they
flouted convention and decency. Antisthenes, an Athenian
disciple of Socrates, founded the sect, which flourished from
400 B.C. The most famous Cynic was Diogenes.

p. 18, ll. 28–30. **and that Plato commended ... known.**
Dionysius the Younger succeeded his father as ruler of
Syracuse in 367 B.C. The 'royal scholar' was culturally
influenced by Plato, who visited Syracuse several times. It is
said that when Dionysius wanted to learn about the constitution of the Athenians, Plato sent him the poetry of
Aristophanes.

p. 18, ll. 31–3. **if holy Chrysostom ... sermon.** St. John
Chrysostom (c. A.D. 345–407), the most eminent father of
the Greek church, was bishop of Antioch and archbishop of
Constantinople. He denounced corruption, and the enemies
he made by his unflinching zeal for reform caused him to be
deposed, arrested and exiled. His use of Aristophanes is
reported in the first printed edition of Aristophanes' plays
(1498).

p. 19, ll. 1–3. **Lycurgus their lawgiver ... Homer.** Lycurgus
(probably ninth century B.C.) remains a shadowy figure in
history, to whom legend ascribes the developments which
occurred in more than two centuries of Spartan life. According to Plutarch, Lycurgus brought Homer's poems from
Asia minor, and 'was the first to make them generally
known'.

p. 19, l. 3. **Thales,** also called Thaletes (probably seventh century B.C.), was a Cretan poet and musician who seems,
despite Plutarch's story, to have lived a century or two after
Lycurgus.

p. 19, l. 9. **Archilochus** (seventh century B.C.) was a lyric and
satiric poet. According to Plutarch, he was banished from
Sparta for writing that it is better to throw away one's shield

than one's life. We have the poem, but the incident is mythical.

p. 19, ll. 14–15. **Euripides affirms . . . unchaste.** Euripides asserts in *Andromache* that 'no Spartan girl could be modest even if she wished'. In Sparta, men and women did gymnastics together in the nude.

p. 19, ll. 19–20. **the pontific college,** the supreme ecclesiastical authority of ancient Rome, managed the complex calendar and religious law as well as ceremonial.

p. 19, ll. 22–7. **Carneades and Critolaus . . . Italy.** Carneades (*c.* 213–129 B.C.) founded a sect of sceptical philosophers in Athens. It was called the New Academy. With Critolaus (head of the Peripatetic school) and Diogenes of Babylonia, a Stoic — not the famous Cynic — he was sent to Rome in 155 B.C. as an ambassador from the Athenians. Young Romans flocked to his two public lectures on justice. In his second, using the technique of the Greek sophists, he refuted all that he had said in his first. Cicero gives the gist of both.

Cato (234–149 B.C.) became censor of Rome in 184 B.C., after a distinguished military career. He vehemently opposed the introduction of Greek sophistication and luxury.

p. 19, l. 27. **Scipio** the Younger (185–129 B.C.) was a leading Roman patron of the Greek culture that Cato attacked.

p. 19, l. 28. **old Sabine austerity.** Cato's father owned a farm in the Sabine country. Life there was simple, rough and old-fashioned.

p. 20, ll. 1–2. **and the censor himself . . . scrupulous.** When he was eighty or more, Cato overcame his scruples and began to learn Greek. (The old man, Sir Philip Sidney suggests, probably feared that the god of the underworld did not understand Latin.)

p. 20, ll. 3–5. **Naevius and Plautus . . . Philemon.** Writers of early Roman comedy copied the Greeks. Naevius wrote his first play in 235 B.C. (eighty years before the embassy of Carneades) and died about 202 B.C. The most popular Roman comedies were by Plautus (*c.* 254–184 B.C.). Menander (342–291 B.C.) and Philemon (*c.* 361–263 B.C.) were renowned Athenian comic dramatists.

p. 20, ll. 7–8. **his unbridled pen . . . recantation.** In his plays,

Naevius satirized Scipio and the famous family of the Metelli.
His recantation took the form of two comedies written in
prison; but he again offended, and he died in exile.

p. 20, ll. 8–9. **we read also … Augustus:** see, for example,
Tacitus' *Annals* I. 72.

p. 20, ll. 13–14. **And therefore Lucretius … Memmius.**
Lucretius dedicated his poem, *De Rerum Natura*, to Caius
Memmius, who was praetor in 58 B.C. The poem, though
passionately anti-religious, does not altogether deny the
existence of the gods, but it attacks degrading conceptions
of them and presents nobly the philosophy of Epicurus.

p. 20, ll. 14–17. **had the honour … writings.** St. Jerome states
Lucretius verse was 'most worthy of Cicero's file', i.e. of
being emended and edited by Cicero. The title of 'pater
patriae' was bestowed on Cicero for having crushed Catiline's
conspiracy of 63 B.C. In his philosophical works, Cicero
combats the doctrines of Epicurus.

p. 20, l. 18. **Lucilius** (*c.* 180–103 B.C.) was the first great Roman
satirist. His verses remain only in fragments. Horace,
Juvenal and Persius regarded him as their master.

    Catullus (87–*c.* 47 B.C.) wrote poems of many sorts and
genuine inspiration. He directed his satire against Julius
Caesar, whose only revenge was to invite the poet and
hospitably entertain him at table.

    Flaccus (65–8 B.C.) is generally known as Horace. (His
full name is Quintus Horatius Flaccus.) His *Satires* expose
the folly rather than the wickedness of vice.

p. 20, ll. 19–20. **the story of Titus Livius … faction.** The
history of Rome by Livy (59 B.C.–A.D. 17) consisted of 142
books, of which 35 still exist. The portion that Milton
refers to described the civil war between the parties of
Pompey and Octavius Caesar: only a brief summary of it
remains. Tacitus mentions that the work was tolerated by
Octavius Caesar, afterwards the Emperor Augustus.

p. 20, l. 22. **Naso** (43 B.C.–A.D. 18) is generally known as Ovid.
(His full name is Publius Ovidius Naso.) When he was aged
forty-three, and apparently in the favour of Augustus, he
was suddenly banished from Rome, ostensibly for being the
author of *Ars Amatoria*. A decade had passed, however,
since he had written that licentious poem, and the real

cause of his exile remains unknown. Augustus' grand-daughter, Julia, was banished at the same time as Ovid.

p. 20, ll. 24–5. **the books were neither . . . called in.** Ovid's books were not suppressed, but *Ars Amatoria* is said to have been removed from the public libraries at the command of Augustus.

p. 20, l. 31. **By this time.** Constantine, the first emperor who publicly professed Christianity, reigned A.D. 306–37.

p. 21, l. 2. **general councils,** as opposed to local ones. Constantine assembled the first general council at Nicaea in 325. It produced the Nicene Creed.

p. 21, l. 5. **Porphyrius,** or Porphyry (A.D. 233–305), was a leading Neoplatonist. His book against Christianity was so powerful that many fathers of the Church wrote replies to it. All copies of the book were ordered to be publicly burnt in 448, and only fragments remain. Porphyry studied under Longinus at Athens and under Plotinus at Rome.

Proclus (A.D. 412–85) was another eminent Neoplatonist and a strong opponent of Christianity. His writings were covered by the edict of Justinian in 529 suppressing the works of Athenian philosophers.

p. 21, l. 7. **a Carthaginian Council:** the fourth, which met in 398.

p. 21, l. 14. **Padre Paolo** (1552–1623), or Paolo Servita, was the religious name taken by Pietro Sarpi when he became a monk. His *History of the Council of Trent* contains a discourse on 'the Prohibition of Books' that greatly influenced *Areopagitica*. His *History of the Inquisition* was also known to Milton, and it probably suggested passages in this work. Elsewhere, Milton calls him 'the great Venetian antagonist of the pope', for championing the republic against papal interference.

p. 21, l. 15. **the Trentine council,** or the Council of Trent, met at intervals between 1545 and 1563. Its decrees were a counterblast to those of the Protestant confession of faith formulated at Augsburg.

p. 21, l. 21. **Martin V** (Otto Colonna, 1368–1431) was pope from 1417.

p. 21, l. 23. **John Wycliffe** (*c.* 1329–84) and John *Hus* (*c.* 1369–1415) were the great English and Bohemian forerunners of the Protestant Reformation. Hus died heroically at the stake for his doctrines.

p. 21, l. 25. Leo X (Giovanni de Medici, 1475–1521) was pope from 1513. His bull of 1515 extended censorship to all writings.

p. 21, ll. 26–7. **the Council of Trent and the Spanish Inquisition engendering together.** The influence of the Council of Trent and the advice of Cardinal Caraffa prompted Paul III, who was pope 1534–49, to increase the power of the Dominican Inquisition over old and new books. Caraffa became Pope Paul IV, and in 1559 he produced the first Roman Index of prohibited books. (Previous indexes had been local.) In 1564, the Tridentine Index modified Paul IV's legislation. The Spanish Index under Philip II, first published in Antwerp — where most heretical books were printed — in 1571, and then in Spain in 1574, was much wider than the Roman.

p. 22, l. 3. **as if St. Peter ... keys.** On the Roman Catholic doctrine of 'the power of the keys, as it is called, or the right of binding or loosing' (as Milton writes in *Christian Doctrine*), see Matthew xvi. 18, 19.

p. 22, l. 15. **this present work of Davanzati.** Bernardo Davanzati Bostichi (1529–1606), a Florentine, wrote an account of the English Reformation. It was printed in 1638, and on the flyleaf of the original edition are the passages here translated. The book may have been published during Milton's stay in Florence.

p. 23, ll. 2–3. **ducking each to other ... reverences.** The licensers of the Inquisition were usually Dominican friars.

p. 23, ll. 8–9. **one from Lambeth House ... Paul's.** The Star Chamber's decree of 1637 entrusted the licensing of books to the Archbishop of Canterbury and the Bishop of London or their substitutes. (*Paradise Lost* was licensed, after hesitation, by the archbishop's chaplain.)

p. 23, l. 27. **no envious Juno sat cross-legged.** When Hercules was about to be born, the goddess Juno, who was jealous of his mother, caused the goddess of delivery to sit cross-legged at the door and so retard his birth for a week. Crossed legs were thought to be a bad omen.

p. 24, ll. 2–3. **Radamanth and his colleagues.** Rhadamanthus, Minos and Aeacus were the three judges in Hades.

NOTES

73

p. 24, ll. 4–5. **that mysterious iniquity:** see Revelation xvii. 1–5. The Puritans equated Babylon with Rome.

p. 24, l. 10. **minorites.** The followers of St. Francis were called Friars Minor ('lesser brethren') as a sign of humility. They were accused, at the Reformation, of proclaiming humility and practising arrogance. The Puritans thought that the chaplains of English bishops were similarly guilty.

p. 24, l. 24. **Lullius,** or Raymond Lull (*c.* 1234–1315), an Italian born in Majorca, was famous for his writings on medicine and chemistry. He went to North Africa to convert the Moslems, but they stoned him to death.

p. 24, l. 29. **as was propounded:** see p. 4, l. 33.

p. 24, l. 32. **'Moses** was learned in all the wisdom of the Egyptians' (Acts vii. 22).

Daniel is one of the four 'children' of whom it is said that 'God gave them knowledge and skill in all learning and wisdom: and Daniel had understanding in all visions and dreams' (Daniel i. 17).

Paul quoted from Greek literature. For examples, see the next note.

p. 25, ll. 2–4. **Paul especially . . . tragedian.** The 'sentences' are:
   i. 'As certain also of your own poets have said, For we are also his offspring' (Acts xvii. 28). This is from Aratus.
   ii. 'Evil communications corrupt good manners' (I Corinthians xv. 33). Milton calls this, in his preface to *Samson Agonistes*, 'a verse of Euripides', but it may have been a Greek proverb.
   iii. 'The Cretans are always liars, evil beasts, slow bellies' (Titus i. 12). This is from Epimenedes.

p. 25, l. 8. **Julian the Apostate** (Flavius Claudius Julianus, A.D. 331–63), nephew to Constantine the Great, was emperor from 361. He was brought up as a Christian, but when he became emperor he declared himself, what he had long been, a pagan. He directly forbade Christians to teach, but some Christians do seem to have sat under pagans.

p. 25, ll. 13–14. **the two Apollinarii,** father and son, were of Alexandria, where the younger was bishop. When Julian the Apostate forbade the Christians to share in Greek culture, the father composed a grammar for Christians and recast the Old Testament in Greek epic and dramatic form.

The son expounded the New Testament in the style of Plato's dialogues.

p. 25, ll. 14–15. **the seven liberal sciences** were the medieval curriculum, comprising the trivium (grammar, logic and rhetoric) and the quadrivium (arithmetic, geometry, astronomy and music).

p. 25, l. 17. **the historian Socrates,** called 'Scholasticus', wrote in the fifth century. His *Ecclesiastical History* is a continuation of the one by Eusebius.

p. 25, ll. 19–20. **with the life . . . it.** Julian's decree was repealed by his successor, Jovian, who was himself a Christian.

p. 25, l. 23. **Decius** Trajanus (A.D. 201–51), who became emperor in 249, and **Diocletian** (A.D. 245–313), who was emperor 284–305, both persecuted the Christians.

p. 25, l. 24. **the same political drift** was the tendency of diabolic diplomacy to undermine the Church by depriving it of classical learning.

p. 25, ll. 24–5. **the devil whipped St. Jerome in a lenten dream.** St. Jerome (*c.* A.D. 340–420) was a scholar and translator of the Bible. To deter his disciple, the nun Eustochium, from reading pagan authors, he wrote a letter (in 384) describing a vision he had when feverish and reduced by fasting in Lent. In the spirit he was brought up for judgement before God. When he professed to be a Christian, a voice cried: 'Thou liest! Thou are a Ciceronian, for the works of that author possess thy heart,' and condemned Jerome to be scourged by angels.

A vision was thought to be a more certain revelation than a dream, and Jerome insisted that the waking nature of his vision was proved by the real whip-marks later found on his body. Milton suggests that the devil, not an angel, chastised the dreaming saint.

p. 25, ll. 30–1. **whom he confesses to have been reading.** Jerome, in his letter, mentions reading Plautus as a relaxation after penance and sleepless nights.

p. 25, l. 34. **Basil** the Great (*c.* A.D. 330–79) was bishop of Caesarea from 370. He wrote rules for monks.

p. 26, l. 1. **Margites** was a mock-heroic poem, of which only four lines remain. Plato and Aristotle attributed it to Homer, but its true authorship is unknown.

p. 26, l. 2. **Il Morgante Maggiore** is a mock-heroic romance by the fifteenth-century Italian poet, Luigi Pulci.

p. 26, l. 5. **Eusebius** Pamphilius (A.D. *c.* 264–*c.* 340) became bishop of Caesarea about 315, thirty years before the birth of St. Jerome. The vision of Dionysius is recorded in Eusebius' *Ecclesiastical History*, the first organized account of the Church. (On the continuation by Socrates Scholasticus, see above, p. 25, l. 17 n.)

p. 26, l. 6. **Eustochium.** Neuter names were not uncommon among women of the fourth century.

p. 26, l. 7. **Dionysius Alexandrinus** (*c.* A.D. 190–265) was bishop of Alexandria.

p. 26, l. 20. **Prove all things . . . good:** see I Thessalonians v. 21.

p. 26, l. 21. **another remarkable saying:** see Titus i. 15.

p. 26, l. 27. **that unapocryphal vision:** see Acts x. 9–16. Milton contrasts this 'unapocryphal vision' with Jerome's 'phantasm'.

p. 27, l. 4. **Mr. Selden.** John Selden (1584–1653) was, like John Pym and John Hampden, an eminent champion of liberty. His *History of Tithes* (1618) greatly offended James I, and Charles I imprisoned him several times for opposition to the royal prerogative. Selden was a lawyer and a most learned man. His 'volume of natural and national laws' was written in Latin and published in 1640. Its English title is: *On Natural Law and the Law of Nations, According to the System of the Hebrews.*

p. 27, ll. 18–19. **when He himself . . . Jews:** see Exodus xvi.

p. 27, ll. 22–3. **For these actions . . . defile not:** see Matthew xv. 11, xv. 17–20, and Mark vii. 14–23.

p. 27, l. 28–9. **Solomon informs us . . . flesh:** see Ecclesiastes xi. 12. Ecclesiastes used to be ascribed to Solomon.

p. 27, l. 33–p. 28, l. 1. **the burning of those Ephesian books . . . magic:** see Acts xix. 19. Ephesus had a reputation for magic.

p. 28, l. 1. **the Syriac . . . them.** The Syriac or Aramaic version, published in 1623, tells of magicians bringing their books.

p. 28, l. 10–12. **those confused seeds . . . asunder.** When Cupid fell in love with Psyche, his mother, Venus, was very angry. She mixed a great heap of various seeds together and commanded Psyche to sort them out. Ants took pity on Psyche and did the work for her. (See *The Golden Ass* by Apuleius, books IV–VI.)

p. 28, l. 22. **warfaring.** The first edition reads 'wayfaring', but in all the four known presentation copies the 'y' is crossed out and an 'r' written above in handwriting that looks like Milton's. The context seems to demand the stronger word.

p. 28, ll. 25–6. **the race where . . . heat:** see I Corinthians ix. 24–5.

p. 28, ll. 33–4. **Spenser, whom I dare . . . teacher.** 'Milton was the poetical son of Spenser', wrote Dryden, and 'Milton has acknowledged to me that Spenser was his original' (*Preface to the Fables*).

p. 28, l. 34. John Duns **Scotus** (*c.* 1270–1308) was an eminent schoolman, a Franciscan. He was born in Scotland or Ireland, and he taught in Oxford and Paris. His thought was influenced by Platonism and he opposed the doctrines of Aquinas.

St. Thomas **Aquinas** (*c.* 1225–74) was the greatest of the schoolmen, a Dominican. He was born in Italy, and he spent his life there except for visits to Cologne and Paris. His philosophy followed Aristotle's. Orthodox Catholic theology is based on the works of Aquinas.

p. 29, ll. 1–3. **describing true temperance . . . bliss:** see *The Faerie Queene*, book II, canto vii, for Sir Guion's descent into the cave of Mammon. The palmer, however, was not with him, as book II, canto viii, stanza 3 makes plain. The bower of bliss is described in book II, canto xii.

p. 29, ll. 16–18. **holiest men . . . Epicurus.** Ecclesiastes, Job and some of the Psalms present strong arguments for the world.

p. 29, ll. 19–22. **ask a Talmudist . . . Chetiv:** ask a Rabbi why he is so squeamish that Moses and all the prophets cannot persuade him to read the holy words, instead of the bowdlerized glosses.

p. 29. ll. 22–3. **the Bible itself . . . books.** Before the Reformation, vernacular versions of the Bible were frowned upon by the Roman Catholic Church. Milton's father, the Protestant son of a Roman Catholic, is said to have been disinherited for reading the Bible.

p. 29, ll. 24–5. **Clement of Alexandria** (second century), the first Church father to make an intimate knowledge of Greek culture serve Christianity, wrote an address to dissuade the Greeks from their old, impure, polytheistic religion.

p. 29, ll. 25–7. **that Eusebian book . . . gospel.** Eusebius (see p. 26, l. 55 n.) wrote *A Preparation for the Gospel*, in which he quotes ancient pagan authors who might have prepared their readers for Christianity.

p. 29, l. 27. **Irenaeus** became bishop of Lyons in 177. His only surviving book is an attack on heresies.

Epiphanius became bishop of Constantia in 367. He wrote an attack on heresies.

p. 29, l. 28. **Jerome**: see p. 25, ll. 24–5 n.

p. 30, l. 6. **Petronius** (*d.* 66) was a favourite of Nero, an aesthete and director of amusements (*arbiter elegantiarum*) at his court.

p. 30, l. 8. **ribald of Arezzo . . . courtiers.** Aretino (1492–1557), who came from Arezzo, was a coarse satirist. His writings were acclaimed and feared in Milan, Florence and Venice.

p. 30, l. 9. **him**: Sir Francis Brian (*d.* 1550), cousin of Anne Boleyn, minor poet and favourite of Henry VIII. Brian's wickedness earned him his nickname, and his wit amused the king.

p. 30, l. 10. **vicar of hell** is a parody of the pope's title, 'Vicar of Christ'.

p. 30, ll. 12–14. **an Indian voyage . . . westward.** Travellers hoped to replace the tedious journey to the Indies with a sea-voyage by an undiscovered passage, either north-east or north-west.

p. 30, ll. 18–19. **those books must . . . licenser,** presumably because such books 'cannot be suppressed without the fall of learning' (p. 31, l. 1). The licensing order was directed specifically at books of religious controversy, and they certainly were not exempt from it.

p. 30, ll. 23–4. **as the prophecy . . . eunuch**: see Acts viii. 27–35.

p. 30, l. 29. **Arminius** (Jacob Hermanus, 1560–1609) was a Dutch theologian. In 1589 he was asked to defend the doctrine of predestination, which had been attacked in some anonymous tracts circulating in Delft. They, however, altered Arminius's own opinion.

perverted. Arminian denial of the doctrine of predestination was favoured by Milton's opponents, Laud and his followers. To Milton, in 1644, such denial seemed corrupt; but later he was converted to Arminianism.

p. 31, l. 28. Aristotle says that political science (the science of a well-ordered life) proves useless to a man who follows the dictates of passion (Ethics I. iii).

Solomon: see Proverbs xxiii. 9.

p. 31, ll. 28–9. our Saviour: see Matthew vii. 6.

p. 32, ll. 7–8. that sainted Inquisition was officially named 'The Sacred Congregation of the Holy Office'.

p. 32, ll. 10–12. and hath almost prevented ... explaining: this third point of my argument (see p. 16, l. 27) has almost anticipated my proofs by becoming evident in the course of what I have already said.

p. 32, ll. 25–6. least of all ... Laws. In his book entitled *Laws*, which was less admired than his other works, Plato depicts a state that Milton considers utopian. Milton goes on to refer to *Laws* VII, which suggests that the whole passage alludes to Plato's *Laws* rather than his *Republic*.

p. 32, l. 30. an Academic night-sitting: a philosophical symposium. Plato taught at the Academia, a public garden near Athens. He and his followers were therefore called the Academic philosophers. Plato's *Symposium* shows a drinking party attended by Socrates, Alcibiades and Aristophanes.

p. 33, l. 6. expelled. Plato was not banished, but after the death of Socrates he did temporarily leave Athens to travel abroad.

p. 33, l. 7. wanton, because they treat of homosexual love.

dialogues: probably the *Symposium* and *Phaedrus*.

p. 33, l. 8. Sophron Mimus. Sophron, the mime writer, lived in Syracuse about 460–420 B.C. Plato is said to have introduced Sophron's mimes, or realistic dramatic sketches, into Athens, and Milton states in his *Apology for Smectymnuus* that Plato used to read them nightly 'and after make them his pillow'.

p. 33, l. 9. Aristophanes: see p. 18, ll. 17–18 n.

p. 33, ll. 9–11. for commending ... Dionysius: see p. 18, ll. 28–30 n.

p. 33, l. 11. his chief friends. Socrates, for instance, is ridiculed in the *Clouds* and Nicias in the *Knights*.

p. 33, l. 27. **Doric** (or Dorian). In *Laws* VII, Plato discusses the
sorts of music to be banned and allowed, but does not use
the names (Dorian, Phrygian, Lydian and Ionian) which he
gives in *Republic* III. Only the manly styles, Dorian and
Phrygian, are to be allowed.

p. 33, ll. 27–30. **There must be . . . provided of.** *Laws* VII. 802.

p. 34, ll. 4–7. **The villages also . . . Mayors.** Milton satirizes
the hated visitations enforced by Laud as archbishop of
Canterbury.

p. 34, l. 5. **lectures.** Puritan sermons were often given by
'lecturers', ordained preachers who were not members of
the parish clergy. Laud objected.

   the bagpipe used to be common in the south of England.

p. 34, l. 7. **Arcadias.** Sir Philip Sidney's *Arcadia*, first printed in
1590, was a very popular romance of chivalry with a pastoral
background.

   Monte Mayors. Jorge e Montemayor's Spanish
romance, *Diana*, based on Sanazzaro's *Arcadia*, was
published about 1559 and became known all over Europe.

p. 34, l. 22. **Atlantic.** In his *Critias*, Plato refers to a sunken
continent, named Atlantis, fabled to have lain west of the
Straits of Gibraltar. Bacon, in his *New Atlantis* (unfinished,
1626), places his imaginary commonwealth on the fictitious
island of Bensalem in the Pacific.

   Utopian. Sir Thomas More describes another ideal
commonwealth in *Utopia* (1516). The name means 'no-
where'.

p. 34, l. 30. **there.** Milton is probably alluding to *Laws* I. 643–4
rather than *Republic* IV. 424–33.

p. 36, l. 22. **that continued court-libel**: *Mercurius Aulicus*
('The Court Mercury'), a virulent Royalist weekly newspaper produced, by Charles I's orders, at Oxford. It consisted of one sheet, sometimes more, and was published
regularly from 1642 to 1645. Secret presses in London
reprinted it.

p. 37, l. 3. **officials.** Laud had sent investigators, known as
'officials', to ecclesiastical courts all over the country, to
examine offenders.

p. 37, ll. 4–5. **that the commonwealth . . . damnified.** Milton
refers to the decree of the Roman senate in critical times:

'dent operam consules ne quid respublica detrimenti capiat'.

p. 37, l. 10. **Trent:** see p. 21, l. 14 n. and p. 21, ll. 26–7 n.

    Seville: where the Spanish Inquisition was formally instituted by Torquemada in 1481.

p. 37, ll. 14–17. **who is so unread . . . traditions?** This idea was widely known because historians frequently used it to explain the lack of documentary evidence.

p. 37, l. 28. **wafted:** floated across the river which, in ancient mythology, divides life from death.

p. 38, l. 4. **in a hand scarce legible.** Milton's own handwriting was beautifully clear.

p. 38, ll. 27–30. **It was the complaint . . . discouraged.** This argument was put forward against the bill for abolishing bishops, deans and chapters, which was debated in Parliament in 1641.

p. 38, l. 28. **pluralities** were abhorred by Milton. He had already written vehemently against them in *Animadversions*.

p. 38, l. 31. **the tenth part** is a reference to tithes.

p. 39, l. 33. **Palladian oil.** The olive tree was sacred to Pallas Athene, goddess of wisdom. Her devotees 'burn the midnight oil'.

p. 41, ll. 5–7. **Sir Francis Bacon that 'such . . . times'.** Bacon discusses, in *An Advertisement Touching the Controversies of the Church of England*, the attempts of bishops to suppress certain pamphlets. 'Forbidden writing', he says, 'is always thought to be certain sparks of a truth that fly up in the faces of those that seek to choke it and tread it out; whereas a book authorized is thought to be but *temporis voces*, the language of the time'. Bacon wrote this in 1589, but it was not published until 1640.

p. 41, ll. 17–18. **though it were Knox . . . spake it.** The 1644 edition of the *History of the Reformation in Scotland* by John Knox (1505–72) seems to have been altered and abridged, but whether by order of licensers or not is unknown.

p. 41, ll. 21–2. **what an author . . . book:** perhaps Knox and his book already referred to, or Sir Edward Coke (1552–1634) and one of the posthumous volumes of his *Institutes* (generally thought to have been mutilated), the last of which appeared in 1644.

p. 41, l. 24. **a more convenient season.** Apparently it never came.

p. 42, l. 8. **twenty.** Six days after the licensing order, Parliament announced thirty-four licensers excluding the Parliamentary Committee for Printing. Perhaps the number was reduced later.

p. 42, l. 13. **monopolized.** The era of the hated monopolies was recent enough to charge the word with loathing.

p. 42, l. 17. **like that imposed . . . Philistines:** see I Samuel xiii. 19–20.

p. 42, ll. 30–1. **whenas debtors and delinquents . . . keeper.** Imprisoned debtors often enjoyed some liberties. 'Delinquents' (all who had helped Charles I) were pardoned on certain conditions in January 1644. Milton's brother, Christopher, seems to have benefited by the relaxation.

p. 43, l. 26. **enchiridion.** Milton, like Erasmus before him, plays on the two meanings.

p. 43, l. 27. **the castle St. Angelo,** which was a papal prison in Milton's time, had been a fortress.

p. 43, ll. 32–3. **when I have sat . . . men.** Milton met learned Italians during his visit to their country in 1638–9.

p. 44, ll. 7–8. **Galileo grown old . . . Inquisition.** Galileo 1564–1642), the great physicist and astronomer, was seventy-four and blind when Milton visited him at his villa near Florence in 1638. The Inquisition restricted Galileo's movements, even after his recantation, for having heretically insisted that the earth revolves round the sun. In *Paradise Lost*, Milton apparently accepts the ancient Ptolmaic system, but also shows his awareness of the modern Copernican system upheld by Galileo.

p. 44, l. 13. **worthies:** Pym, Hampden and other prominent members of the Long Parliament.

p. 44, l. 20. **in time of Parliament.** There had been no Parliament between 1629 and 1640.

p. 44, ll. 22–3. **he whom an honest quaestorship . . . Sicilians.** Cicero held the financial position of a quaestor in Sicily in 75 B.C. He was respected and popular.

p. 44, l. 24. **by them importuned against Verres,** who was praetor in Sicily, 73–71 B.C., and who desolated the island by his extortions. When his term of office ended, the

G

Sicilians indicted him. They entrusted their case to Cicero, who therefore composed his Verrine orations: the first two were enough to drive Verres into exile.

p. 45, l. 2. **leaf.** Milton puns on the two meanings.

p. 45, l. 3. **who but of late . . . silenced:** Presbyterian ministers who, not long before, had been hardly allowed to preach.

p. 45, l. 6. **a second tyranny:** see p. 2, l. 6 for the first tyranny, that of the Stuarts and the prelacy.

p. 45, ll. 7–8. **bishops and presbyters . . . thing.** Puritans, insisting that the gospel recognizes no ecclesiastical order except priest and deacon, argued against episcopacy 'that a bishop and presbyter is all one both in name and office'. (The word 'priest' comes from 'presbyter'.) Milton bitterly suggests now that bishop and presbyter will soon be considered 'all one' in evil practice, too, with the new presbyters as bad as the old bishops.

p. 45, ll. 15–16. **sole ordination . . . parishioner.** In the Smectymnuan controversy Milton had already attacked the bishop's claims to these sole rights.

p. 45, l. 20. **Covenants.** The Scots' National Covenant (1638) expressed opposition to Charles I and Laud in Scotland. It was the basis of the Solemn League and Covenant (ratified by Parliament in 1643), which bound the Scottish army to help the Long Parliament and undertook to abolish episcopacy and to reform religion in England upon the Scottish model.

Protestations. In 1641, the Commons drew up a Protestation that it would uphold religion, Crown, Parliament and 'the lawful rights and liberties of the subjects'.

p. 46, ll. 10–11. **the cruse of truth . . . oil:** see I Kings xvii. 9–16.

p. 46, ll. 16–18. **this obstructing violence . . . drives at.** The cruel sentences inflicted by the Star Chamber on Prynne and others during the 1630s had caused public indignation.

p. 46, l. 20. **'The punishing of wits . . . authority'.** Milton translates the quotation from Tacitus included by Bacon in *An Advertisement Touching the Controversies of the Church of England*: 'punitis ingeniis gliscit auctoritas'.

p. 46, ll. 21–3. **'and a forbidden . . . out'.** For Milton's previous use of this quotation see p. 41, ll. 5–7 n.

p. 46, l. 29. **in scripture:** see Song of Solomon iv. 15, which was allegorically interpreted, and Psalms lxxxv. 11.

p. 47, l. 6. **an implicit faith** was considered adequate for the lower clergy and the laity of the medieval Church, who were expected to accept doctrines that they did not understand.

p. 47, l. 7. **Loretto,** in central Italy, was a centre of medieval superstition. Pilgrims flocked there to see the house in which the Virgin was born. The belief that angels had flown it from Palestine was mocked by Protestant scoffers.

p. 47, l. 26. **malmsey.** Wine was a normal early-morning drink.

p. 47, l. 28. **green figs:** see Matthew xxi. 17–19 and Mark xi. 12–14.

p. 48, l. 1. **the tunnaging and the poundaging.** Before the Long Parliament met, the country had been aroused by Charles I's attempts to collect this lucrative revenue of three shillings on each tun (barrel) of wine and one shilling in the pound (of value) on all other goods imported.

p. 48, ll. 22–3. **doctrinal heads, uses, motives, marks and means** were the sections from which sermons were built.

p. 49, ll. 1–2. **St. Thomas ... St. Martin and St. Hugh.** Milton ironically uses the names of mundane shopping-centres as if they were the names of churches, notorious for the sale of sermons and other merchandise.

our London trading St. Thomas: the part of Cheapside rich in mercers' shops, close to the Mercers' Chapel of St. Thomas.

vestry. Perhaps Milton puns on the ecclesiastical 'vestry' and the secular 'vestiary', a place where clothes were kept.

St. Martin: the disreputable market for beads, lace and copper-ware in the precincts of St. Martin le Grand.

St. Hugh: the area frequented by shoemakers, Cordwainers' Ward. In London there was no church dedicated to St. Hugh, but he was associated with shoemakers.

p. 49, l. 26. **Christ urged it:** see John xviii. 19–20.

p. 50, ll. 15–16. **the Turk upholds ... printing.** Printing was not allowed in Turkey until 1723.

p. 50, l. 22. **mortal glass:** see I Corinthians xiii. 12.

p. 50, ll. 29–35. **as that story goes ... could find them.** The legend is that Typhon murdered his brother Osiris, cut the body into pieces and threw them into the Nile. The widowed Isis searched for the severed remains of her husband and eventually found them. Plutarch, whose version Milton probably adopted, insisted that the legend should be taken as an allegory.

p. 50, l. 30. **the good Osiris** had civilized the barbarous Egyptians.

p. 51, ll. 10–12. **those planets . . . sun.** Venus and Mercury are planets frequently 'combust'. Venus is known as Hesperus, the evening star, and as Lucifer, the morning star.

p. 51, l. 22. **Zuinglius:** Ulrich Zwingli (1484–1531), of Zürich, who began the Reformation in Switzerland.

Calvin: John Calvin (1509–64), the Genevan reformer, whose doctrines were more uncompromising than Zwingli's.

p. 51, l. 33. **the golden rule** in arithmetic is a method of solving problems about numbers in proportion.

p. 52, ll. 10–11. **writers of good antiquity . . . judgement,** such as Justin Lipsius (1547–1606), a Flemish humanist, and Michael Drayton (1563–1631), the English poet.

p. 52, l. 12. **the school of Pythagoras.** Drayton, in his *Polyolbion*, ascribes to the Druids the Pythagorean doctrine of the transmigration of souls. Milton also alludes here to a Norman building in Cambridge known as the School of Pythagoras.

the Persian wisdom: the art of magic, which Pliny the Elder suggests the Persians might have learnt from the British.

p. 52, l. 14. **Julius Agricola** was proconsul in Britain from A.D. 78 to 85 and governed for three Caesars. He introduced the policy of educating the sons of the British nobles, and valued the natural talents of the Britons more highly than the learning of the Gauls.

p. 52, ll. 16–20. **Nor is it for nothing . . . arts.** Transylvania, now part of Romania, was independent from 1535 to 1689, and staunchly Protestant. Many of her theologians came to study at the Protestant universities of the West.

p. 52, l. 18. **the Hercynian wilderness** is a translation of Hercynia Silva, the name given by Julius Caesar to the mountains and forests of central and southern Germany.

p. 52, ll. 24–5. **as out of Sion:** see Joel ii. 1.

p. 52, l. 28, l. 29. **Wycliffe** and **Hus:** see p. 21, l. 23 n.

p. 52, l. 30. **Jerome** of Prague (*c.* 1365–1416) was, like Hus, a Bohemian reformer who was burnt for his faith.

Martin **Luther** (1483–1546) was the Saxon peasant and Augustinian monk who initiated the Reformation in Germany.

Calvin: see p. 51, l. 22 n.

p. 53, ll. 9–10. **the shop of war ... waking.** This was the year of the battles of Marston Moor and Newbury. Breast-plates were almost the only armour worn.

p. 53, l. 20. **a nation of prophets:** see Numbers xi. 27–9.

p. 53, l. 21. **more than five months ... harvest:** see John iv. 35, where there 'are yet four months'. I do not know why Milton changed four to five.

p. 53, ll. 32–3. **a little forbearance ... another:** see Ephesians iv. 2.

p. 54, l. 6. **as Pyrrhus did** in 280 B.C. when, as king of Epirus, he invaded Italy, defeated the Romans at Heraclea and exclaimed: 'How easy it would be for me to seize the empire of the world with Roman soldiers, or for the Romans to seize it with me as king!'

p. 54, l. 11. **while the temple ... building:** see I Kings v and vi.

p. 54, ll. 25–30. **wherein Moses ... envy them:** see Numbers xi. 27–9 and p. 53, l. 20 n.

p. 55, ll. 8–11. **when a city ... trenches.** During the previous summer, 1643, trenches were dug round London as a twelve-mile circuit of defence against the Royalist soldiers, who advanced to the suburbs after the battle of Edgehill in October 1643.

p. 55, ll. 21–3. **when Rome was nigh ... rate,** in 211 B.C. The story is told by Livy (XXVI. 11).

p. 56, l. 5. **her invincible locks,** like Samson's in Judges xvi.

p. 56, l. 15. **twenty:** see p. 42, l. 8 n.

p. 57, l. 6. **an abrogated and merciless law** gave Roman fathers the right to kill their children. It had fallen into disuse long before its abolition in A.D. 318.

p. 57, l. 9. **coat and conduct** was the name of a military tax that had been levied on the counties. In the Grand Remonstrance, 1641, the Long Parliament had petitioned to remove it.

four nobles. A noble was worth 6s. 8d.

Danegeld was a tax imposed originally to protect England against the Danes. When John Hampden refused to pay ship-money and was tried in 1636, the Counsel for the Crown cited Danegeld as a precedent for Charles I's levy.

p. 57, ll. 17–20. **one of your own ... commonwealth.** Robert Greville, second Lord Brook (1608–43), one of the leaders of the Parliamentary party in the House of Lords, and a general in the Parliamentary army, was killed while commanding an attack at Lichfield. In his *Discourse of Episcopacy* he prays for 'the unity of the Spirit in the bond of peace'.

p. 57, l. 28. **who bequeathed ... disciples:** see John xiv. 15–31, especially 21 and 27.

p. 58, ll. 6–7. **The temple of Janus ... open.** The Temple of Janus, the two-faced Roman god of doors, was open during war and shut during peace.

p. 58, ll. 7–8. **all the winds of doctrine:** see Ephesians iv. 14–15.

p. 58, ll. 19–21. **to use diligence ... late:** see Proverbs ii. 4–5.

p. 59, ll. 4–6. **the old Proteus ... bound.** Proteus, the old, reluctant prophet-god in Greek myth, eluded capture by changing his shape. If and when he was caught he told the truth.

p. 59, ll. 7–8. **as Micaiah ... Ahab:** see I Kings xxii. 1–36.

p. 59, l. 13. **that handwriting ... cross:** see Colossians ii. 14.

p. 59, ll. 14–15. **which Paul so often boasts of,** especially in Romans and Galatians.

p. 59, l. 21. **a linen decency.** Puritans hated all vestments and wore black gowns instead of surplices.

p. 59, ll. 30–1, l. 35–p. 60, l. 1. **wood and hay stubble** and **gold and silver and precious stones:** see I Corinthians iii. 10–13.

p. 60, ll. 1–3. **it is not possible ... things:** see Matthew xiii. 24–30 and 36–43.

p. 60, l. 16, l. 17. **unity of Spirit** and **bond of peace:** see Ephesians iv. 3.

p. 60, ll. 33–5. **when God shakes ... reforming:** see Haggai ii. 7.

p. 61, ll. 12–14. **one while in the old ... Westminster.** Convocation, the general assembly of the national clergy, met in the chapter-house at Westminster from Wolsey's time until the end of Laud's. Its powers, with some additions, were transferred by the Long Parliament to the Assembly of Divines which met in Henry VII's chapel in Westminster.

p. 61, ll. 14–15. **when all the faith ... canonized.** The Assembly was working on a catechism, a confession of faith, a directory of worship and a frame of Church-government, all of which the Presbyterians intended Parliament to establish.

p. 61, ll. 19–20. **Harry VII himself ... about him.** Henry VII and many other monarchs were buried in the chapel where the Assembly met.

p. 62, ll. 15–16. **the check that Moses ... Joshua:** see p. 54, ll. 25–30. n.

p. 62, ll. 16–17. **the countermand which ... John:** see Luke ix. 49–50.

p. 62, ll. 23–4. **the most Dominican ... Inquisition:** see p. 23, ll. 2–3.

p. 62, ll. 30–1. **that Order published ... this:** see Introduction, p. 3. Milton quotes from the Order of 29 January 1642. Two more Orders were, however, issued between that and the Licensing Order, and Milton is almost certain to have been aware of them both. For the purposes of his argument, Milton presumably needed to hide the fact that the Long Parliament had continuously intended to replace the Star Chamber decree by restrictions on the liberty of the press. He represents the Licensing Order as a sudden and grim sign of the dangerous power of the Assembly of Divines — a warning to the Presbyterians in Parliament, with whom alone lay hope for a repeal of the Licensing Order. They might force a repeal if they could be sufficiently alarmed at the prospect of England becoming a theocracy. Milton had provided numerous reminders of Laud's regime in *Areopagitica*.

p. 63, l. 1. **Spanish:** see p. 18, l. 6 n.

p. 63, l. 4. **a Star Chamber decree** of 11 July 1637. See Introduction, p. 3.

p. 63, l. 6. **for which she is now fallen.** The Court of Star Chamber was abolished in 1641.

p. 63, ll. 6–7. **with Lucifer:** see Isaiah xiv. 12.

p. 63, l. 11. **your precedent Order:** see p. 62, ll. 30–1 n.

p. 63, ll. 15–17. **the poor in their Company ... copy:** see p. 16, ll. 20–2 n.

OF EDUCATION

Introduction

I. THE BACKGROUND

1. IDEAS ABOUT EDUCATION

EDUCATION always interested Milton, and educational reform was in the air when he wrote his tractate. The current system did not satisfy thinkers who wanted education to fulfil the demands of Christian humanism and of practical life, and many English works on educational reform were written between 1530 and 1660. When Milton wrote *Of Education*, in 1644, Bacon's criticisms and suggestions were being echoed by men who wished to modernize the aims and methods of schools and universities. Three years before, in 1641, the House of Commons had resolved to devote confiscated lands to education, and London was then the centre of remarkable schemes for educational advance on an international scale. Two of the most visionary reformers were John Amos Comenius of Bohemia, whose works are mentioned in the tractate, and his disciple Samuel Hartlib, for whom Milton wrote it.

Although the schemes of 1641, which were some of the most exciting of the age, had not materialized, and Comenius had left England, Hartlib's friendship with both men ensured that Milton was in touch with advanced ideas on education in 1644. Milton acknowledges that his tractate is influenced by 'old renowned authors', but disclaims special knowledge of contemporary theories. *Of Education* is not part of any particular movement, although it is in the main stream of enlightened humanist reform and may have been considerably influenced by *De Tradendis Disciplinis*, a book by the sixteenth-century Spaniard, Juan Luis Vives.

Milton's ideas about education seem to have arisen primarily out of his own agreeable experience of enlightenment at St. Paul's School and his disagreeable experience of obscurantism at Cambridge. Renaissance educational thought enriched those ideas, but all that Milton adopted he made truly his own.

He plans to finish his students' formal education not at a university but at his ideal school. The background of dissatisfaction with universities can be traced to Bacon's criticisms in *De Augmentis* (1623); but far more potent influences on Milton's thought were his own Cambridge experiences of scholastic logic and metaphysics, which had made university education for him 'an asinine feast of sow-thistles and brambles'. In the tractate, he makes his students' cultural work reach its climax with the enlightened exercises which need maturity: composition in verse and prose. Those were the exercises that he himself excelled in. And when, unconventionally, mathematics and music are emphasized in the tractate, the warrant for them is to be found not so strongly in Plato as in the personal enthusiasm of Milton who, as a young graduate, came to London from the seclusion of Horton for lessons in mathematics and music. His educational scheme can be linked with the theories of his predecessors and his contemporaries, but he built it on strong personal beliefs that arose from his own passionate loves and hates.

2. SAMUEL HARTLIB

Of Education is addressed to 'Master Hartlib'. About eight or ten years older then Milton, Samuel Hartlib was born in Prussia of Polish and English stock. With his third wife, who was English, he settled in London as a merchant about 1628. Milton may have first met him in 1643, or earlier.

Among the favourite schemes of Hartlib — a public-spirited idealist with immensely wide interests — were those for uniting all the Protestant Churches of Europe and for improving education. His educational ideas, expounded in various publications, were greatly influenced by those of Comenius, a Moravian theologian and educational theorist who was about ten years his senior. No man tried more ardently than Hartlib to gain English support for the ideas and projects of Comenius.

Hartlib invited at least nine educationalists to write treatises, most of which he then published. *Of Education* was written at his request. In conversation, Hartlib evidently found Milton eager for reform; and yet the tractate *Of Education*, though solicited by Hartlib and addressed to him, does not seem to have been one of his acknowledged publications. The reason for this is uncertain.

Perhaps Milton's views, developed on paper, surprised and dis-
appointed Hartlib by their radical divergence from those of
Comenius. Certainly the allusion to 'many modern Januas and
Didactics', the works of Comenius, lacks enthusiasm, and the
tractate may have been rejected by Hartlib and published by
Milton instead.

3. MILTON AS SCHOOLMASTER

Milton's nephews, his sister's sons, Edward and John Phillips,
were his first pupils. Edward left accounts of Milton's six years'
practice as a schoolmaster, and they are an important and reveal-
ing part of the background to the tractate *Of Education*.

In 1640, when Edward was ten, his mother and stepfather sent
him to Milton for daily lessons. At the same time his brother
John, aged nine, went as an adopted son and pupil to live with
Milton 'at Mr. Russell's, a tailor in St. Bride's churchyard ...'.
Edward goes on to say that in a year's time Milton 'made them
capable of interpreting a Latin author at sight; and within three
years they went through the best of Latin and Greek poets,
Lucretius and Manilius of the Latins; Hesiod, Aratus, Dionysius
Afer, Oppian and Quintus Calaber'. John Aubrey (presumably
on the authority of Edward Phillips) adds to the list of achievements 'the use of the globes', 'some rudiments of arithmetic and
geometry' and 'Apollonii Argonautica', and states that 'Cato,
Varro and Columella *De Re Rustica* were the very first authors
they learnt'.

Milton's first wife 'oft-times heard his nephews cry, and
beaten', according to Aubrey's *Minutes of the Life of Mr. John
Milton* (from which the quotations above are taken). It also
states, however, that 'as he was severe on one hand, so he was
most familiar and free in his conversation to those to whom most
severe in his way of education — N.B. He made his nephews
songsters, and sing from the time they were with him'.

Edward Phillips's account in his own *Life* of Milton is fuller
than the *Minutes* that he helped Aubrey to compile. 'I judge it
not impertinent', Edward writes about Milton's teaching,

'to mention the many authors both of the Latin and Greek,
which through his excellent judgment and way of teaching, far
above the pedantry of common, public schools (where such

authors are scarce ever heard of) were run over within no greater compass of time than from ten to fifteen or sixteen years of age.

'Of the Latin: the four grand authors, *De Re Rustica*, Cato, Varro, Columella and Palladius; Cornelius Celsus, an ancient physician of the Romans; a great part of Pliny's *Natural History*; Vitruvius his *Architecture*; Frontinus his *Stratagems*; with the two egregious poets, Lucretius and Manilius.

'Of the Greek: Hesiod, a poet equal with Homer; Aratus his *Phaenomena*, and *Diosemeia*; Dionysius Afer *De Situ Orbis*; Oppian's *Cynegetics* and *Halieutics*; Quintus Calaber his poem of the Trojan war continued from Homer; Apollonius Rhodius his *Argonautica*; and in prose, Plutarch's *Placita Philosophorum*, and Περι Παιδων 'Αγωγιας; Geminus' *Astronomy*; Xenophon's *Cyri Institutio*, and *Anabasis*; Aelian's *Tactics*; and Polyaenus his *Warlike Stratagems*. . . .

'Nor did the time thus studiously employed in conquering the Greek and Latin tongues, hinder the attaining to the chief oriental languages, *viz.* the Hebrew, Chaldee and Syriac, so far as to go through the Pentateuch, or five books of Moses in Hebrew, to make a good entrance into the Targum, or Chaldee paraphrase, and to understand several chapters of St. Matthew in the Syriac Testament; besides an introduction into several arts and sciences, by reading Urstisius his *Arithmetic*, Riff's *Geometry*, Petiscus his *Trigonometry*, Joannes de Sacro Bosco *De Sphaera*; and into the Italian and French tongues, by reading in Italian, Giovan Villani's *History of the Transactions* between several petty states of Italy; and in French a great part of Pierre Davity, the famous geographer of France in his time.

'The Sunday's work was for the most part the reading each day a chapter of the Greek Testament, and hearing his learned exposition upon the same. . . . The next work after this, was the writing from his own dictation some part, from time to time, of a tractate which he thought fit to collect from the ablest of divines, who had written of that subject; Amesius, Wollebius, etc. . . .

'Now persons so far manuducted into the highest paths of literature both divine and human, had they received his documents with the same acuteness of wit and apprehension, the same industry, alacrity, and thirst after knowledge as the instructor was endued with, what prodigies of wit and learning might they have proved! The scholars might in some degree have come near to the equalling of the master. . . .'

Edward Phillips approves of Milton's example of 'hard study, and spare diet' and insists that Milton

'never set up for a public school to teach all the young fry of a parish, but only was willing to impart his learning and knowledge to relations, and the sons of some gentlemen that were his intimate friends; besides, that neither his converse, nor his writings, nor his manner of teaching ever savoured in the least anything of pedantry; and probably he might have some prospect of putting in practice his academical institution, according to the model laid down in his sheet *Of Education*. The progress of which design was afterwards diverted by a series of alteration in the affairs of State. . . .'

Edward Phillips's enthusiastic account is a tribute to the purpose, integrity and drive of Milton the teacher, who used in his original little school many of the ideas that he presents in the tractate.

II. *OF EDUCATION*

The tractate *Of Education* is essentially a letter rather than a pamphlet, and like all good letters it creates a vivid image of the writer. Milton the idealist appears in its few pages as the planner of a boarding-school education for able boys: his feet are on the ground, but his head is above the clouds gazing towards a vision of the righteous, enlightened, learned, practical leader of Englishmen — the system's perfect product. In the tractate the centuries unite, so that, for instance, Greek example and England's immediate need both prompt Milton to insist on elaborate military training.

John Phillips calls Milton's educational scheme 'easy and delightful', and the simple, fresh style and breezy tone of the tractate do make the description seem appropriate. Milton is right in thinking that learning should be a pleasant occupation. The great scholar's own enthusiasm convinces us, while we read, that his schoolboys too will be full of exuberant eagerness to master the host of prescribed subjects, will delight in the exercises he suggests and thrive on the 'diet' he briefly advises.

Erasmus expected schoolboys to read as many Greek and Latin authors as Milton recommends, and the most famous European schools fulfilled Erasmus's expectations: but Milton plans a vast curriculum to develop the boys' powers in a remarkably logical and realistic order. The beginning of the syllabus shows the process clearly, and its fusion of ideal and practical is representative of the whole course. As Masson says: 'Given a lofty and varied idea of utility, no man has ever been more strenuously utilitarian than Milton in this tract.'

The boys would come to Milton's school able to read and write, and they would then be taught Latin grammar. Next, to develop their Latin (the language of textbooks on all subjects), and to instil a proper attitude towards the whole process of education, Milton would have enlightened moral works by classical authors read to the boys. Mathematics would begin at this stage.

A true knowledge of God is, Milton believes, the aim of learning, but mankind must study basic, concrete things first and then ascend, in education, the great chain of being that leads to God. (This progress from things to ideas is in accord with the philosophy of Milton's time and with the educational psychology of ours.) Now that the preliminary studies are complete, Milton therefore sets his pupils to read standard works about the world around them, beginning with the books on agriculture that enlightened English gentleman-farmers in that age would study. His remark that this may lead to improved national farming is typical of Milton the patriot, who hopes that his system will attract foreign students and be copied abroad.

Greek is now started, and the syllabus widens. The most inquisitive, versatile and energetic boy, taught by the practical experts wisely recommended by Milton, might be satisfied by a fraction of the courses on geography, astronomy, zoology, botany, architecture, meteorology, mineralogy, mathematics, fortification, engineering and navigation that Milton prescribes. Out of the comprehensive list, few subjects could be mastered by any one student; but, although Milton recognizes variety of aptitude, he wants each boy to study a very wide syllabus.

Milton, who had been a genius of a schoolboy, bought his fabulous scholarship at the cost of his eyesight. His nephews and his other pupils, none of them geniuses, were toiling through a massive curriculum with sweat and occasional tears while he wrote his tractate. (The young Earl of Barrimore, perhaps — as Anthony à Wood suggests — because 'the tempers of our gentry would not bear the strictness' of Milton's discipline, could not stay the course.) But the imaginary boy, fit for the schooling planned in the tractate, was a super-pupil, a student made in Milton's own image and, heir to the qualities of Castiglione's courtier, was worthy of being bred to the highest Renaissance calling, that of the enlightened ruler equipped for peace and war.

Those sorts of modern education that stem from the Renaissance concept of the magnanimous, versatile leader of men can obviously gain rich nourishment from the tractate. But so can all sorts of education, for this little work with its provocative assumptions and challenging definitions is wider than any one tradition — wider, indeed, than all systems. In the tractate, Milton discusses 'education in a summary manner, but sufficiently copious for those who attend seriously to the subject; than which nothing can be more necessary to principle the minds of men in virtue', as he declares in *Defensio Secunda*. He only discusses the education of one class, ignores the education of girls, and plans a school that has still not been founded and never will be: yet the light that shines from the tractate can illuminate our thoughts about education and make our teaching and our learning shine too.

We need this light now. It is the light of faith in the power of knowledge — knowledge neither as an end in itself nor as a mundane qualification, but as a means of attaining true life. It is the light of faith in the infinite capacity of the human mind directed aright. And it is the light of faith in mankind's ability to benefit from the freedom into which education should liberate the human spirit.

Of Education

TO MASTER SAMUEL HARTLIB

MASTER HARTLIB,

I am long since persuaded that to say and do aught worth memory and imitation, no purpose or respect should sooner move us than simply the love of God and of mankind. Nevertheless, to write now the reforming of education, though it be one of the greatest and noblest designs that can be thought on, and for the want whereof this nation perishes, I had not yet at this time been induced but by your earnest entreaties and serious conjurements; as having my mind diverted for the present in the pursuance of some other assertions, the knowledge and the use of which cannot but be a great furtherance both to the enlargement of truth and honest living with much more peace.

Nor should the laws of any private friendship have prevailed with me to divide thus or transpose my former thoughts; but that I see those aims, those actions which have won you with me the esteem of a person sent hither by some good providence from a far country to be the occasion and incitement of great good to this island, and (as I hear) you have obtained the same repute with men of most approved wisdom and some of the highest authority among us; not to mention the learned correspondence which you hold in foreign parts, and the extraordinary pains and diligence which you have used in this matter both here and beyond the seas, either by the definite will of God so ruling, or the peculiar sway of nature, which also is God's working.

Neither can I think that, so reputed and so valued as you are, you would, to the forfeit of your own discerning ability, impose

13 *divide:* divert. 14–15 *won you with me . . . person:* won my esteem for you as a person. 21 *this matter:* 'the reforming of education'. 23 *nature:* your own nature.

upon me an unfit and over-ponderous argument; but that the satisfaction, which you profess to have received from those incidental discourses which we have wandered into, hath pressed and almost constrained you into a persuasion, that what you require from me in this point I neither ought nor can in conscience defer beyond this time, both of so much need at once, and so much opportunity to try what God hath determined.

I will not resist, therefore, whatever it is either of divine or human obligement that you lay upon me; but will forthwith set down in writing, as you request me, that voluntary idea, which hath long in silence presented itself to me, of a better education, in extent and comprehension far more large, and yet of time far shorter and of attainment far more certain, than hath been yet in practice. Brief I shall endeavour to be; for that which I have to say assuredly this nation hath extreme need should be done sooner than spoken. To tell you, therefore, that I have benefited herein among old renowned authors I shall spare; and to search what many modern Januas and Didactics more than ever I shall read have projected, my inclination leads me not. But if you can accept of these few observations which have flowered off, and are, as it were, the burnishing of many contemplative years altogether spent in the search of religious and civil knowledge, and such as pleased you so well in the relating, I here give you them to dispose of.

The end, then, of learning is, to repair the ruins of our first parents by regaining to know God aright, and out of that knowledge to love him, to imitate him, to be like him, as we may the nearest, by possessing our souls of true virtue, which, being united to the heavenly grace of faith, makes up the highest perfection. But because our understanding cannot in this body found itself but on sensible things, nor arrive so clearly to the knowledge of God and things invisible as by orderly conning over the visible and inferior creature, the same method is necessarily to be followed in all discreet teaching.

7 *try:* test. 10 *idea* in the Platonic as well as the general sense.
23 *relating:* telling. 31 *sensible things:* things that can be apprehended by the senses. 34 *discreet:* judicious.

H

And seeing every nation affords not experience and tradition enough for all kind of learning, therefore we are chiefly taught the languages of those people who have at any time been most industrious after wisdom; so that language is but the instrument conveying to us things useful to be known. And though a linguist should pride himself to have all the tongues that Babel cleft the world into, yet if he have not studied the solid things in them as well as the words and lexicons, he were nothing so much to be esteemed a learned man as any yeoman or tradesman competently wise in his mother-dialect only.

Hence appear the many mistakes which have made learning generally so unpleasing and so unsuccessful. First, we do amiss to spend seven or eight years merely in scraping together so much miserable Latin and Greek as might be learned otherwise easily and delightfully in one year. And that which casts our proficiency therein so much behind is our time lost in too oft idle vacancies given both to schools and universities; partly in a preposterous exaction, forcing the empty wits of children to compose themes, verses and orations, which are the acts of ripest judgment, and the final work of a head filled, by long reading and observing, with elegant maxims and copious invention.

These are not matters to be wrung from poor striplings, like blood out of the nose, or the plucking of untimely fruit; besides the ill habit which they get of wretched barbarizing against the Latin and Greek idiom with their untutored Anglicisms, odious to be read, yet not to be avoided without a well-continued and judicious conversing among pure authors, digested, which they scarce taste. Whereas, if after some preparatory grounds of speech by their certain forms got into memory they were led to the praxis hereof in some chosen short book lessoned thoroughly to them, they might then forthwith proceed to learn the substance of good things and arts in due order, which would bring

17 *vacancies:* holy-days, on which boys did no ordinary school work. 18 *preposterous exaction:* premature demand. 19 *themes:* essays. 21 *elegant:* correct. 27 *well-continued:* sustained. 28 *conversing:* consorting. 31 *praxis:* practice. 33 *arts:* sorts of knowledge.

the whole language quickly into their power. This I take to be the most rational and most profitable way of learning languages, and whereby we may best hope to give account to God of our youth spent herein.

And for the usual method of teaching arts, I deem it to be an old error of universities, not yet well recovered from the scholastic grossness of barbarous ages, that, instead of beginning with arts most easy (and those be such as are most obvious to the sense), they present their young unmatriculated novices at first coming with the most intellective abstractions of logic and metaphysics; so that they, having but newly left those grammatic flats and shallows where they stuck unreasonably to learn a few words with lamentable construction, and now on the sudden transported under another climate, to be tossed and turmoiled with their unballasted wits in fathomless and unquiet deeps of controversy, do, for the most part, grow into hatred and contempt of learning, mocked and deluded all this while with ragged notions and babblements, while they expected worthy and delightful knowledge; till poverty or youthful years call them importunately their several ways, and hasten them, with the sway of friends, either to an ambitious and mercenary, or ignorantly zealous divinity: some allured to the trade of law, grounding their purposes not on the prudent and heavenly contemplation of justice and equity, which was never taught them, but on the promising and pleasing thoughts of litigious terms, fat contentions, and flowing fees. Others betake them to state affairs with souls so unprincipled in virtue and true generous breeding, that flattery, and court-shifts, and tyrannous aphorisms appear to them the highest points of wisdom, instilling their barren hearts with a conscientious slavery, if, as I

8 *obvious to the sense:* concrete.   9 *unmatriculated:* undeveloped. 10 *intellective:* intellectual.   19 *youthful years:* the impatience of youth. 22 *divinity:* ordination.   23 *prudent:* based on jurisprudence, the philosophy of law.   25–6 *litigious terms:* periods when the courts are in session.   *fat contentions:* lucrative cases.   27 *state affairs:* statesmanship.   28 *court shifts:* political trickery.   *tyrannous aphorisms:* maxims justifying tyranny.   30 *conscientious slavery:* servility based on misdirected loyalty.

rather think, it be not feigned. Others, lastly, of a more delicious
and airy spirit, retire themselves, knowing no better, to the
enjoyments of ease and luxury, living out their days in feast and
jollity; which, indeed, is the wisest and safest course of all these,
unless they were with more integrity undertaken. And these are
the errors, and these are the fruits of mis-spending our prime
youth at the schools and universities, as we do, either in learning mere words, or such things chiefly as were better unlearnt.

I shall detain you no longer in the demonstration of what we
should not do, but straight conduct you to a hillside, where I
will point you out to the right path of a virtuous and noble
education; laborious indeed at the first ascent, but else so
smooth, so green, so full of goodly prospect and melodious
sounds on every side, that the harp of Orpheus was not more
charming. I doubt not but ye shall have more ado to drive our
dullest and laziest youth, our stocks and stubs, from the infinite
desire of such a happy nurture, than we have now to haul and
drag our choicest and hopefullest wits to that asinine feast of
sow-thistles and brambles which is commonly set before them
as all the food and entertainment of their tenderest and most
docible age. I call, therefore, a complete and generous education, that which fits a man to perform justly, skilfully, and
magnanimously all the offices, both private and public, of peace
and war. And how all this may be done between twelve and
one-and-twenty, less time than is now bestowed in pure trifling
at grammar and sophistry, is to be thus ordered:

First, to find out a spacious house and ground about it fit for
an academy, and big enough to lodge one hundred and fifty
persons, whereof twenty or thereabout may be attendants, all
under the government of one who shall be thought of desert
sufficient, and ability either to do all, or wisely to direct and
oversee it done. This place should be at once both school and
university, not needing a remove to any other house of scholar-

1 *delicious:* voluptuous.   2 *airy:* sanguine; of the temperament associated with the element, air.   6 *prime youth:* youth at its best.   15
charming: full of musical and magical power.   16 *stocks and stubs:* logs
and tree-stumps.   21 *docible:* teachable.   25 *pure:* mere.   29 *attendants:* assistant masters.

ship, except it be some peculiar college of law or physic, where they mean to be practioners; but as for those general studies which take up all our time from Lily to the commencing, as they term it, master of art, it should be absolute. After this pattern, as many edifices may be converted to this use as shall be needful in every city throughout this land, which would tend much to the increase of learning and civility everywhere. This number, less or more, thus collected, to the convenience of a foot-company or interchangeably two troops of cavalry, should divide their day's work into three parts as it lies orderly — their studies, their exercise, and their diet.

For their studies: first, they should begin with the chief and necessary rules of some good grammar, either that now used, or any better; and while this is doing, their speech is to be fashioned to a distinct and clear pronunciation, as near as may be to the Italian, especially in the vowels. For we Englishmen, being far northerly, do not open our mouths in the cold air wide enough to grace a southern tongue, but are observed by all other nations to speak exceeding close and inward; so that to smatter Latin with an English mouth is as ill hearing as law French.

Next, to make them expert in the usefullest points of grammar, and withal to season them and win them early to the love of virtue and true labour, ere any flattering seducement or vain principle seize them wandering, some easy and delightful book of education should be read to them, whereof the Greeks have store, as Cebes, Plutarch, and other Socratic discourses; but in Latin we have none of classic authority extant, except the two or three first books of Quintilian and some select pieces elsewhere.

But here the main skill and groundwork will be to temper them such lectures and explanations upon every opportunity, as may lead and draw them in willing obedience, inflamed with

1 *peculiar:* special. 3 *Lily:* the Latin grammar written by Lily. *commencing:* taking the full degree. 7 *civility:* good citizenship. 8 *to the convenience of:* as would be suitable for. 9 *interchangeably:* alternatively. 10 *as:* so that. 20 *smatter:* talk ignorantly. 23 *season:* train. 24 *flattering:* beguiling. 31 *temper:* devise for.

the study of learning and the admiration of virtue, stirred up
with high hopes of living to be brave men and worthy patriots,
dear to God and famous to all ages: that they may despise and
scorn all their childish and ill-taught qualities, to delight in
manly and liberal exercises; which he who hath the art and
proper eloquence to catch them with, what with mild and
effectual persuasions, and what with the intimation of some
fear, if need be, but chiefly by his own example, might in a short
space gain them to an incredible diligence and courage, infusing
into their young breasts such an ingenuous and noble ardour as
would not fail to make many of them renowned and matchless
men.

At the same time, some other hour of the day might be
taught them the rules of arithmetic, and, soon after, the
elements of geometry, even playing, as the old manner was.
After evening repast till bed-time their thoughts would be best
taken up in the easy grounds of religion and the story of Scripture.

The next step would be to the authors of agriculture, Cato,
Varro and Columella, for the matter is most easy; and if the
language is difficult, so much the better; it is not a difficulty
above their years. And here will be an occasion of inciting and
enabling them hereafter to improve the tillage of their country,
to recover the bad soil, and to remedy the waste that is made of
good; for this was one of Hercules' praises.

Ere half these authors be read (which will soon be with plying
hard and daily) they cannot choose but be masters of an
ordinary prose: so that it will be then seasonable for them to
learn in any modern author the use of the globes and all the maps,
first with the old names and then with the new; or they might
then be capable to read any compendious method of natural
philosophy; and, at the same time, might be entering into the
Greek tongue, after the same manner as was before prescribed

1 *study of:* zeal for.   5 *liberal:* gentlemanly.   10 *ingenuous:* high-
minded.   15 *playing:* by mathematical games.   17 *of:* on.   29 *globes*
of sky and earth, to teach astronomy as well as geography.   31 *natural
philosophy:* science.

for the Latin; whereby the difficulties of grammar being soon overcome, all the historical physiology of Aristotle and Theophrastus are open before them and, as I may say, under contribution. The like access will be to Vitruvius, to Seneca's *Natural Questions*, to Mela, Celsus, Pliny or Solinus. And having thus past the principles of arithmetic, geometry, astronomy, and geography, with a general compact of physics, they may descend in mathematics to the instrumental science of trigonometry, and from thence to fortification, architecture, enginery, or navigation. And in natural philosophy they may proceed leisurely from the history of meteors, minerals, plants, and living creatures, as far as anatomy.

Then also in course might be read to them out of some not tedious writer the institution of physic; that they may know the tempers, the humours, the seasons, and how to manage a crudity; which he who can wisely and timely do is not only a great physician to himself and to his friends, but also may at some time or other save an army by this frugal and expenseless means only, and not let the healthy and stout bodies of young men rot away under him for want of this discipline, which is a great pity, and no less a shame to the commander.

To set forward all these proceedings in nature and mathematics, what hinders but that they may procure, as oft as shall be needful, the helpful experiences of hunters, fowlers, fishermen, shepherds, gardeners, apothecaries; and in other sciences, architects, engineers, mariners, anatomists, who, doubtless, would be ready, some for reward and some to favour such a hopeful seminary. And this would give them such a real tincture of natural knowledge as they shall never forget, but daily

2 *historical physiology:* natural science arranged systematically. 3 *under contribution:* made to contribute to their knowledge. 7 *compact of physics:* treatise on natural science. 8 *descend:* go on from general principles to specific applications. 10 *enginery:* engineering. 11 *history of meteors:* systematic study of meteorology. 14 *institution of:* introduction to. *physic:* medicine. 15 *tempers:* general aspects of bodily constitution. *humours:* basic physical qualities. *seasons:* effects of the seasons on health. 16 *crudity:* imperfect state of the humours. 20 *discipline:* learning. 29 *natural knowledge:* natural science and its uses.

augment with delight. Then also those poets which are now counted most hard will be both facile and pleasant, Orpheus, Hesiod, Theocritus, Aratus, Nicander, Oppian, Dionysius; and, in Latin, Lucretius, Manilius, and the rural part of Virgil.

By this time, years and good general precepts will have furnished them more distinctly with that act of reason which in ethics is called proairesis, that they may with some judgment contemplate upon moral good and evil. Then will be required a special reinforcement of constant and sound endoctrinating to set them right and firm, instructing them more amply in the knowledge of virtue and the hatred of vice, while their young and pliant affections are led through all the moral works of Plato, Xenophon, Cicero, Plutarch, Laertius, and those Locrian remnants; but still to be reduced in their nightward studies, wherewith they close the day's work, under the determinate sentence of David or Solomon, or the evangels and apostolic scriptures.

Being perfect in the knowledge of personal duty, they may then begin the study of economics. And either now or before this they may have easily learned at any odd hour the Italian tongue. And soon after, but with wariness and good antidote, it would be wholesome enough to let them taste some choice comedies, Greek, Latin, or Italian; those tragedies also that treat of household matters, as Trachiniae, Alcestis, and the like.

The next move must be to the study of politics; to know the beginning, end, and reasons of political societies, that they may not, in a dangerous fit of the commonwealth, be such poor shaken uncertain reeds, of such a tottering conscience as many of our great councillors have lately shown themselves, but steadfast pillars of the State. After this they are to dive into the grounds of law and legal justice, delivered first and with best warrant by Moses, and, as far as human prudence can be trusted, in those extolled remains of Grecian lawgivers, Lycurgus, Solon, Zaleucus, Charondas; and thence to all the

7 *proairesis:* choice.　14 *reduced:* led back.　15 *determinate sentence:* definitive wisdom.　16 *evangels:* gospels.　19 *economics:* social duty. 24 *household:* domestic.　27 *fit:* crisis.

Roman edicts and tables, with their Justinian; and so down to the Saxon and common laws of England and the statutes.

Sundays also and every evening may now be understandingly spent in the highest matters of theology and church history, ancient and modern: and ere this time at a set hour the Hebrew tongue might have been gained, that the Scriptures may be now read in their own original; whereto it would be no impossibility to add the Chaldee and the Syrian dialect.

When all these employments are well conquered, then will the choice histories, heroic poems, and Attic tragedies of stateliest and most regal argument, with all the famous political orations, offer themselves; which, if they were not only read, but some of them got by memory, and solemnly pronounced with right accent and grace, as might be taught, would endue them even with the spirit and vigour of Demosthenes or Cicero, Euripides or Sophocles.

And now, lastly, will be the time to read with them those organic arts which enable men to discourse and write perspicuously, elegantly, and according to the fitted style of lofty, mean or lowly. Logic, therefore, so much as is useful, is to be referred to this due place, with all her well-couched heads and topics, until it be time to open her contracted palm into a graceful and ornate rhetoric taught out of the rule of Plato, Aristotle, Phalereus, Cicero, Hermogenes, Longinus.

To which poetry would be made subsequent, or indeed rather precedent, as being less subtle and fine, but more simple, sensuous, and passionate; I mean not here the prosody of a verse which they could not but have hit on before among the rudiments of grammar, but that sublime art which in Aristotle's Poetics, in Horace, and the Italian commentaries of Castelvetro, Tasso, Mazzoni, and others, teaches what the laws are of a true epic poem, what of a dramatic, what of a lyric, what decorum is, which is the grand masterpiece to observe. This would make

8 *Chaldee:* Aramaic. *Syrian:* Syriac. 18 *organic:* creative. 19 *fitted:* apt. 20 *mean:* plain. *lowly:* colloquial. 22 *topics:* arguments. 25 *or indeed rather precedent:* although it takes precedence because of its nature. 33 *masterpiece:* most important feature.

them soon perceive what despicable creatures our common rhymers and playwriters be; and show them what religious, what glorious and magnificent use might be made of poetry, both in divine and human things.

From hence, and not till now, will be the right season of forming them to be able writers and composers in every excellent matter, when they shall be thus fraught with an universal insight into things: or whether they be to speak in parliament or council, honour and attention would be waiting on their lips. There would then appear in pulpits other visages, other gestures, and stuff otherwise wrought, than we now sit under, ofttimes to as great a trial of our patience as any other that they preach to us.

These are the studies wherein our noble and our gentle youth ought to bestow their time in a disciplinary way from twelve to one-and-twenty, unless they rely more upon their ancestors dead than upon themselves living. In which methodical course it so is supposed they must proceed by the steady pace of learning onward, as at convenient times for memory's sake to retire back into the middle ward, and sometimes into the rear, of what they have been taught, until they have confirmed and solidly united the whole body of their perfected knowledge, like the last embattling of a Roman legion. Now will be worth the seeing what exercises and recreations may best agree and become those studies.

THEIR EXERCISE

The course of study hitherto briefly described is, what I can guess by reading, likest to those ancient and famous schools of Pythagoras, Plato, Isocrates, Aristotle, and such others, out of which were bred such a number of renowned philosophers, orators, historians, poets, and princes all over Greece, Italy,

10 *visages:* facial expressions. 11 *stuff otherwise wrought:* material otherwise arranged. 12–13 *ofttimes to as great . . . to us:* one sermon of this sort being as trying as another. 20 *middle ward:* second military line. 23 *last embattling:* final marshalling.

and Asia, besides the flourishing studies of Cyrene and Alexandria. But herein it shall exceed them, and supply a defect as great as that which Plato noted in the commonwealth of Sparta. Whereas that city trained up their youth most for war, and these in their academies and Lyceum all for the gown, this institution of breeding which I here delineate shall be equally good both for peace and war. Therefore, about an hour and a half ere they eat at noon should be allowed them for exercise, and due rest afterwards; but the time for this may be enlarged at pleasure, according as their rising in the morning shall be early.

The exercise which I command first is the exact use of their weapon, to guard, and to strike safely with edge or point. This will keep them healthy, nimble, strong, and well in breath; is also the likeliest means to make them grow large and tall, and to inspire them with a gallant and fearless courage; which, being tempered with seasonable lectures and precepts to make them of true fortitude and patience, will turn into a native and heroic valour, and make them hate the cowardice of doing wrong. They must be also practised in all the locks and gripes of wrestling, wherein Englishmen are wont to excel, as need may often be in fight to tug, to grapple, and to close. And this, perhaps, will be enough wherein to prove and heat their single strength.

The interim of unsweating themselves regularly, and convenient rest before meat, may both with profit and delight be taken up in recreating and composing their travailed spirits with the solemn and divine harmonies of music heard or learned, either whilst the skilful organist plies his grave and fancied descant in lofty fugues, or the whole symphony with artful and unimaginable touches adorn and grace the well-studied chords of some choice composer; sometimes the lute or soft organ-stop, waiting on elegant voices either to religious, martial, or civil ditties, which, if wise men and prophets be not extremely

5 *the gown:* peaceful occupations. 29 *fancied:* fanciful. 30 *descant:* improvisation. *symphony:* musical assembly. 33 *waiting on:* accompanying.

out, have a great power over dispositions and manners to smooth and make them gentle from rustic harshness and distempered passions. The like also would not be unexpedient after meat, to assist and cherish nature in her first concoction, and send their minds back to study in good tune and satisfaction.

Where having followed it under vigilant eyes until about two hours before supper, they are, by a sudden alarum or watchword, to be called out on their military motions, under sky or covert, according to the season, as was the Roman wont; first on foot, then, as their age permits, on horseback to all the art of cavalry; that having in sport, but with much exactness and daily muster, served out the rudiments of their soldiership in all the skill of embattling, marching, encamping, fortifying, besieging, and battering, with all the helps of ancient and modern stratagems, tactics, and warlike maxims, they may, as it were out of a long war, come forth renowned and perfect commanders in the service of their country.

They would not then, if they were trusted with fair and hopeful armies, suffer them for want of just and wise discipline to shed away from about them like sick feathers, though they be never so oft supplied; they would not suffer their empty and unrecruitable colonels of twenty men in a company to quaff out or convey into secret hoards the wages of a delusive list and miserable remnant; yet in the meanwhile to be overmastered with a score or two of drunkards, the only soldiery left about them, or else to comply with all rapines and violences. No, certainly, if they knew aught of that knowledge which belongs to good men or good governors, they would not suffer these things.

But to return to our own institute. Besides these constant exercises at home, there is another opportunity of gaining experience to be won from pleasure itself abroad: in those

1 *out:* mistaken. 3 *distempered:* disordered, because of unbalanced humours. 4 *first concoction:* first stage of digestion. 7 *it:* study. 10 *covert:* cover. 22 *supplied:* supplied with soldiers. 23 *unrecruitable:* incapable of getting recruits. *quaff out:* drink away. 24 *delusive list:* falsified muster-roll. 27 *comply with:* consent to.

vernal seasons of the year, when the air is calm and pleasant, it were an injury and sullenness against nature not to go out and see her riches and partake in her rejoicing with heaven and earth. I should not, therefore, be a persuader to them of studying much then, after two or three years that they have well laid their grounds, but to ride out in companies with prudent and staid guides to all the quarters of the land, learning and observing all places of strength, all commodities of building and of soil for towns and tillage, harbours, and ports for trade. Sometimes taking sea as far as to our navy, to learn there also what they can in the practical knowledge of sailing and sea-fight.

These ways would try all their peculiar gifts of nature, and if there were any secret excellence among them, would fetch it out and give it fair opportunity to advance itself by, which could not but mightily redound to the good of this nation, and bring into fashion again those old admired virtues and excellences, with far more advantage now in this purity of Christian knowledge.

Nor shall we then need the monsieurs of Paris to take our hopeful youth into their slight and prodigal custodies, and send them over back again transformed into mimics, apes, and kekshose. But if they desire to see other countries at three or four and twenty years of age, not to learn principles, but to enlarge experience and make wise observation, they will by that time be such as shall deserve the regard and honour of all men where they pass, and the society and friendship of those in all places who are best and most eminent. And perhaps then other nations will be glad to visit us for their breeding, or else to imitate us in their own country.

Now, lastly, for their diet there cannot be much to say, save only that it would be best in the same house; for much time else would be lost abroad, and many ill habits got; and that it should be plain, healthful, and moderate, I suppose is out of controversy.

Thus, Mr. Hartlib, you have a general view in writing, as

8 *places of strength:* strongholds. *commodities:* suitabilities. 20 *slight and prodigal:* trifling and extravagant. 22 *kekshose:* fantastic people.

your desire was, of that which at several times I had discoursed with you concerning the best and noblest way of education; not beginning, as some have done, from the cradle, which yet might be worth many considerations, if brevity had not been my scope. Many other circumstances also I could have mentioned; but this, to such as have the worth in them to make trial, for light and direction may be enough. Only I believe that this is not a bow for every men to shoot in that counts himself a teacher, but will require sinews almost equal to those which Homer gave Ulysses. Yet I am withal persuaded that it may prove much more easy in the assay than it now seems at distance, and much more illustrious: howbeit not more difficult than I imagine; and that imagination presents me with nothing but very happy and very possible according to best wishes, if God have so decreed, and this age have spirit and capacity enough to apprehend.

8 *shoot in:* shoot with.   11 *assay:* trial.   14 *but very:* but what is very.

Notes

p. 96, l. 1. **Master Hartlib:** see Introduction, p. 90.

p. 96, l. 10. **some other assertions** were about divorce.

p. 97, l. 7. **much opportunity** was provided by the resolution of the House of Commons in 1641 'that all the lands, taken ... from the deans and chapters, shall be employed to the advancement of learning and piety'.

p. 97, l. 18. **Januas and Didactics.** *Janua Linguarum Reserata*, by John Amos Comenius (1592–1670), was a book of a thousand everyday phrases and sentences in Latin, with translations into the vernacular, intended to teach the reading of Latin and at the same time to convey useful knowledge. It dispensed with formal grammar. First published in 1631, the *Janua* was famous: it had been translated into sixteen foreign languages and had entered its sixth English edition by 1644. Milton, who is bound to have know what sort of work the *Janua* was, may have doubted its value.

The Great Didactic, though already written in Czech, was neither translated into Latin nor published until thirteen years after Milton's tractate. Hartlib had, however, published in England three versions, two in Latin and one in English, of a short synopsis of the work. Probably Milton read the synopsis at Hartlib's instigation, but in this passage he seems to dissociate himself from the doctrines of Comenius.

Comenius came to London in September 1641, hoping to found a college of universal knowledge. He stayed with Hartlib. There is no evidence that Milton knew Hartlib then or ever met Comenius, who abandoned all hope of England's realizing his scheme and left in June 1642, for Sweden, where he was invited to draw up a system of national schooling.

p. 98, l. 19. **themes.** Milton's schoolboy essay, in Latin, *On Early Rising*, is his earliest prose known to exist. He wrote

it when he was fifteen or sixteen, towards the end of his
time at St. Paul's.

p. 98, l. 21. **elegant maxims** should, Milton implies, be chosen
by students themselves for their commonplace books.
There were published collections of 'elegant maxims'.

p. 98, ll. 21–2. **copious invention** included the discovery of
ideas and arguments, and the various ways of expressing
them.

p. 100, l. 14. **the harp of Orpheus** was a symbol of culture.
Orpheus, probably mythical, was a poet and a philosopher,
as well as a singer who could charm all creatures.

p. 100, ll. 24–6. **between twelve . . . sophistry.** Boys generally
entered grammar school, able to read and write English, at
the age of seven, and stayed there until they were fourteen.
They then spent four years working for a B.A. and three
years more for an M.A. Milton's scheme would similarly
end when the pupils were twenty-one, but it would last
only nine years instead of fourteen.

p. 101, l. 3. William **Lily** (*c.* 1468–*c.* 1523), first high-master of
St. Paul's School, wrote a Latin grammar in collaboration
with Colet and Erasmus. Henry VIII ordered it to be used
exclusively. Milton as a schoolboy studied the revised
version of 1574, of which fifteen editions appeared before
1640.

p. 101, l. 9. **a foot company or . . . two troops of cavalry**
comprised about 150 men. The master and boys were
sometimes to drill as infantry and sometimes as cavalry.

p. 101, l. 10. **their day's work** would presumably begin, as in
contemporary grammar schools, at 6 a.m. There would be a
midday break (of more than the two hours enjoyed by
grammar schools) for exercise, a meal and a rest with
music. Then work would be resumed, followed by two
hours of military drill, supper, religious teaching and bed.
In the spring, the older boys would replace formal study
by travel and observation.

p. 101, l. 14. **or any better.** The publication of grammars to
replace Lily's authorized one had not yet led to their general
use. The date of Milton's own Latin grammar in English,
Accedence Commenc't Grammar, is unknown. It was not
published until 1669, and his only other school textbook, a

NOTES   113

treatise on logic, in Latin, was published three years after
that.

p. 101, ll. 15–16. **as near as . . . Italian.** Milton omitted pronunciation from his *Accedence Commenc't Grammar* 'since
few will be persuaded to pronounce Latin otherwise than
their own English'.

p. 101, ll. 20–1. **law French,** though forbidden, was still in
use. Milton, in his *Commonplace Book,* calls it 'Norman
gibberish'.

p. 101, l. 27. **Cebes, Plutarch and other Socratic discourses**
were intended by Milton to be studied in Latin translations.

    Cebes, a pupil and friend of Socrates, was thought to
have written *The Table,* a moral allegory.

    Plutarch (*c.* A.D. 46–after 120) was thought to have
written *On the Education of Children.* Milton's nephews
read it in Greek.

    other Socratic discourses may be parts of Plato's
Republic and *Laws,* and Plutarch's dialogues, *Moralia.*

p. 101, l. 29. **Quintilian** (first century A.D.) discusses his general
theories of education in the first book of *Institutio Oratoria.*
The second book is about oratory, and the third is a subtle
analysis of causes.

p. 102, ll. 14–15. **the rules of arithmetic . . . geometry.** Milton's
introduction of mathematics as early as this seems to be
unique among his contemporaries, and the emphasis he lays
on a thorough study of the subject is very advanced.

p. 102, l. 15. **even playing . . . manner was.** Plato and
Quintilian advocate learning by playing, a method that
Plato says the Egyptians invented.

p. 102, ll. 19–20. **Cato, Varro and Columella.** The standard
Latin books on agriculture were written by Cato the
Censor (234–149 B.C.), Varro (116–27 B.C.) and Columella
(first century A.D.), and they were often combined into one
publication.

p. 102, l. 25. **one of Hercules' praises.** Manuring technique was
thought to have been introduced into Italy with the dung
that Hercules removed from the Augean stables.

p. 102, l. 30. **the old names . . . new.** Some maps used Latin
names, some used vernacular names, and some used a
mixture.

I

p. 103, l. 2. **Aristotle** (384–322 B.C.) wrote on zoology in *Historia Animalium*, *De Partibus Animalium*, *De Incessu Animalium* and *De Generatione Animalium*.

Theophrastus, the pupil and successor of Aristotle, wrote two works on botany, the *Enquiry* and the *Aetiology*.

p. 103, l. 4. **Vitruvius** (first century B.C.) wrote *De Architectura*, a treatise on all aspects of architecture. The last book of the treatise is about military machines.

Seneca (*c.* 5 B.C.–A.D. 65) wrote on meteorology in *Naturales Questiones*.

p. 103, l. 5. **Mela** (first century A.D.) wrote *De Chorographica*, a geographical survey.

Celsus (first century A.D.) wrote an encyclopedia of which only the sections on medicine, and fragments on other subjects, have been preserved.

Pliny the Elder (A.D. 23/4–79) wrote *Naturalis Historia*, a work on geography, biology, mineralogy and other subjects.

Solinus (third century A.D.) wrote *Collectanea Rerum Memorabilium*, a geography book based on the works of Pliny and Mela.

p. 103, l. 7. **astronomy** was studied by Milton's nephews from books on the Ptolemaic system. No book on Copernican astronomy is recommended in the tractate *Of Education*.

p. 104, l. 2. **Orpheus**, the mythical Greek poet, was wrongly thought to have written *Lithica*, a poem on precious stones which was suitable for schoolboys at this stage in Milton's plan.

p. 104, l. 3. **Hesiod**, the second Greek poet chronologically, wrote *Works and Days*, a poem on farming.

Theocritus (third century B.C.) wrote *Idyls*, from which pastoral poetry had developed.

Aratus (third century B.C.) wrote *Phaenomena*, a poem on astronomy.

Nicander (second century B.C.) wrote *Theriaca*, a poem about poisonous creatures and remedies for their bites, and *Alexipharmaca*, a poem about all sorts of poisons and their antidotes.

Oppian (second century A.D.) wrote *Cynegetica*, a poem about hunting, and was thought to have written *Halieutica*, a poem about fishing.

Dionysius (about A.D. 300) wrote *Periegesis*, a geographical poem.

p. 104, l. 4. **Lucretius** (*c.* 94–55 B.C.) wrote *De Rerum Natura*, a a poem presenting the Epicurean view of the universe.

Manilius (first century A.D.) wrote *Astronomica*, a poem on astronomy and astrology.

the rural part of Virgil: the *Eclogues* and the *Georgics*.

p. 104, l. 5. **By this time** the boys would be about fifteen or sixteen years old.

p. 104, l. 7. **proairesis** is the term that Aristotle uses in his definition of moral virtue, to denote voluntary action founded on reasoning.

p. 104, ll. 12–13. **the moral works of Plato** perhaps included the *Apology*, *Crito*, *Phaedo* and *Philebus*.

p. 104, l. 13. **Xenophon** (*c.* 430–*c.* 354 B.C.): perhaps including the *Apology for Socrates*, *Memorabilia*, *Symposium* and *Cyropaedia*.

Cicero (106–43 B.C.): chiefly *De Officiis*, which was used as a standard work on ethics, and perhaps also *De Amicitia* and *De Finibus*.

Plutarch: *Moralia*, perhaps especially the parts entitled *De Virtute Morali*, *De Fraterno Amore* and *De Amore Prolis*.

Laertius (second or third century A.D.) was thought to have written *Lives and Opinions of Eminent Philosophers*.

p. 104, ll. 13–14. **those Locrian remnants**: *On the Soul of the World and Nature* was wrongly attributed to Timaeus of Locri, the main speaker in Plato's *Timaeus*.

p. 104, l. 24. **Trachiniae**, by Sophocles (*c.* 496–406 B.C.), and **Alcestis**, by Euripides (485?–406? B.C.), both show devoted wives.

p. 104, l. 33. **remains**: accounts given by later writers.

p. 104, l. 34. **Lycurgus**, the legendary giver of laws to Sparta, is said by Plutarch to have put none of them into writing. Xenophon 'extolled' Lycurgus highly.

Solon (*c.* 640–*c.* 561 B.C.) remodelled the constitution of Athens.

Zaleucus (seventh century B.C.) produced a legal code, said to have been the earliest written in Europe, for Italian Locri.

Charondas (probably sixth century B.C.) composed laws for Catana in Sicily. They were adopted by other Greek colonies.

p. 105, l. 1. **tables**: the Twelve Tables, drawn up in 450 B.C., which embodied the first Roman legal code.

Justinian (Emperor of the East 527–65) appointed jurists to draw up a complete body of Roman civil law for Europe.

p. 105, l. 5. **at a set hour**, in contrast to learning Italian 'at any odd hour'.

p. 105, ll. 5–6. **the Hebrew tongue** was taught in few schools, but Milton may have learnt it at St. Paul's.

p. 105, l. 15. **Demosthenes** (384–322 B.C.) and **Cicero** were the great Athenian and Roman orators.

p. 105, l. 16. **Euripides** and **Sophocles** were two of the three great Athenian tragic poets.

p. 105, l. 18. **organic arts** are used as instruments.

p. 105, l. 23. **Plato** (*c.* 429–347 B.C.) showed, in *Gorgias* and *Phaedrus*, how rhetoric could be made to serve truth and virtue.

Aristotle, in his *Rhetoric*, taught propriety of style.

p. 105, l. 24. **Phalereus** (*c.* 345–283 B.C.) was thought to have written a treatise *On Style* which is now ascribed to a later writer.

Cicero wrote *De Oratore* and *Orator*.

Hermogenes of Tarsus (second century B.C.) wrote various works on rhetoric.

Longinus (third century A.D.) was thought to have written *On the Sublime*, one of the most important pieces of literary criticism in antiquity.

p. 105, ll. 28–9. **among the rudiments of grammar.** Prosody is the last subject taught in Lily's grammar.

p. 105, ll. 29–30. **Aristotle's Poetics**, which is mainly about tragedy, deals briefly with epic.

p. 105, l. 30. **Horace** discusses drama at length in *Ars Poetica*.

Castelvetro (1505–71), who translated Aristotle's *Poetics* into Italian, developed the doctrine of the three dramatic unities.

p. 105, l. 31. **Tasso** (1544–97) wrote discourses on heroic and other poetry.

Mazzoni (1548–98) wrote defences of Dante's work.

p. 106, l. 29. **Pythagoras** (sixth century B.C.) founded a religious and philosophical brotherhood at Crotona in Italy. Similar Pythagorean societies were formed elsewhere.

    Plato taught for forty years at the Academia outside Athens.

    Isocrates (436–338 B.C.) taught rhetoric for a short time at Chios, and afterwards for about forty years at Athens.

    Aristotle taught from about 335 to 343 B.C. in the Lyceum at Athens.

p. 107, l. 1. **Cyrene** was a centre of mathematical study in the fourth century B.C.

    Alexandria, with its great library and museum, was a centre of literary and scientific study in the last three centuries B.C.

p. 107, l. 3. **as that which Plato . . . Sparta.** The defects of Spartan government are exposed in Plato's *Laws* I.

p. 107, l. 21. **wrestling,** the ancient English sport, had recently been discussed in various works on education.

p. 107, l. 28. **music** was mentioned by few contemporary writers on education.

p. 107, ll. 33–4. **martial . . . ditties** would be songs to inspire disciplined valour.

p. 107, l. 34. **wise men,** such as Plato, Aristotle and Quintilian.

p. 108, l. 8. **supper** was generally between seven and eight o'clock.

p. 108, l. 9. **military** training of this thorough and elaborate sort, to be undertaken in conjunction with liberal studies, is recommended by no contemporary English writer on education.

p. 108, l. 21. **to shed away . . . feathers.** Many soldiers deserted from Essex's army in 1643.

p. 109, l. 12. **their peculiar gifts of nature.** Aptitudes had been mentioned in very few Renaissance works on education.

p. 109, l. 19. **the monsieurs of Paris.** Of Milton's visit to France in 1638 John Phillips, the anonymous early biographer, says: 'In this kingdom, the manners and genius of which he had in no admiration, he made small stay'.

p. 110, ll. 9–10. **those which Homer gave Ulysses: see** *Odyssey* XXI.

Critical Extracts

AREOPAGITICA

I

THE truth, in fact, is that the *Areopagitica* is, in the totality of its argument, unique in its period, and perhaps unequalled in the range of freedom it demands until the *Liberty* of John Stuart Mill, more than two centuries later. It was, of course, written by one whose original Calvinism was permeated by a humanist outlook which binds him, through the central tradition of the great Elizabethan age, to the world of the European Renaissance, and, through its influence, to a culture that is at least as much Greek as Puritan in its inner essence. When we look among the men of Milton's age for kindred views, we must remember how few could hope to enjoy the advantages that had been opened to him. The son of a wealthy father, enjoying at once the privilege of long years of leisure and the experience of foreign travel, driven on by the passionate ambition to create something 'which the world would not willingly let die', preparing himself for the twenty years before the *Areopagitica* appeared, to traverse a vast field of secular learning, he approached the issues of the Civil War from an angle, and with advantages, that few men on the Puritan side could hope to rival. . . .

What he proposed in the *Areopagitica* was a method of determining social relationships which, even yet, the world has not been able to accept. He desired to replace the use of power by the influence of persuasion. He urged men to put their trust in reason as the single solvent of their difficulties. There is a sense, indeed, in which Milton's tract is, above all, a majestic hymn to the power of truth to prevail over falsehood in the battle of ideas. He insists, almost, that, given the free play of the market, truth is bound to prevail. And this leads him to what is virtually the function of a defence of philosophic anarchism in the realm of ideologies, partly on the ground that a 'cloistered virtue' is a worthless thing if it has not emerged victorious over temptation,

and partly because, in a 'free and open encounter', it is the ver-
dict of history, as he affirms, that no one has ever known 'Truth
put to the worse' even 'though all the winds of doctrine were let
loose to play upon the earth'.

It would be insolent to praise the gorgeous tapestry of rhetoric
that Milton wove in defence of his plea. Whole phrases of his
tract have become a part of the classic heritage of free men. It
is not, I think, excessive to say that there are not a dozen
documents in the history of mankind that breathe a nobler
ardour for liberty. Few men have written more splendidly in
defence of the free mind; none has even rivalled that splendour
in defence of the right to keep the mind in chains.

By Harold J. Laski

From *The Areopagitica of Milton after 300 Years*, published in *Freedom of Expression, a Symposium*, edited by
Hermon Ould (Hutchinson, 1945)

II

The speech which Milton addressed to the Parliament of
England in 1644, 'for the Liberty of Unlicensed Printing', was
provoked by the particular circumstances of the time. Those
circumstances had their pattern in the past, most notably in the
Spanish Inquisition: but Milton could not have foreseen that
they would recur in the future, and that three hundred years
after the appearance of his pamphlet, his words would be as apt
as if they had come hot from the press. The *Areopagitica* is
Milton's greatest prose work, and this rank is given to it on
account of its inherent qualities of fervour and style: but it is
great also because of its wisdom, its logic and the universal
application of its argument. Every newly established tyranny
brings its pages to life again: there is no encroachment on 'the
liberty to know, to utter and to argue freely' which it does not
anticipate, and oppose with unanswerable reason.

By Herbert Read

From *On Milton's Areopagitica*, published in *Freedom of
Expression, a Symposium*, edited by Hermon Ould
(Hutchinson, 1945)

III

Areopagitica is the best of Milton's English prose works, because it expresses more of his mind than any other. It is also the summit of one period of his development, comparable to *Lycidas*, which was at once the crowning poem of Milton's youth and the promise of what ought to have followed. Not only does *Areopagitica* express more of Milton's mind: it is more economical in the expression; there is relatively little waste. Fortunately few Scriptural passages bear on the question of the liberty of the press; and Milton was spared the uncongenial task of text-hunting. *Areopagitica* is an organism through most of which the blood circulates freely.

In one way *Areopagitica* is Milton's chief song of hope: in it he has uttered most of the few surviving fragments of the epic which I have supposed him to have contemplated at the beginning of the struggle between Parliament and Royalists, the Song of Innocence that never got written. But in another way it shows a maturity of experience quite new in Milton: a definite development of ideas towards *Paradise Lost*. Although pieces of the Arthuriad may have got themselves expressed, it must have been about the time Milton wrote *Areopagitica* that he abandoned any idea of writing such a poem. *Areopagitica* is thus of special interest in looking both back and forward.

There is much in common between *Areopagitica* and the anti-episcopal pamphlets: the Renaissance tone, the instinct for action, the defence of schisms, and the immense hope of speedy national reformation. The flowery comparison of himself to Isocrates and the appeal to the authority of Plato, who is this time explained away as he happens to be on the wrong side, are in a typically Renaissance manner. The whole plea that the free publishing of books is founded on freedom and width of choice is instinct with the notion that life is worthless without activity, and the more valuable as it is more active.

By E. M. W. Tillyard

From *Milton* (Chatto and Windus, 1930)

OF EDUCATION AND AREOPAGITICA

In the interim he wrote his *Tractate of Education* (1644) and the *Areopagitica* (1644), products of the spirit of the earlier tracts, the spirit of one who still hoped for a reform of reformation, a new Church and a new State. Again, both those tracts must be read as documents of a prophetic rather than a purely practical character. Nothing is easier than to indicate the impracticable character of Milton's scheme of education, which has more than all the faults of most schemes which ignore the fact that very few people can be educated beyond a strict limit. Yet there are one or two things to be noted in the tract. In the first place, his conception of education is comprehensive — intellectual, artistic, physical. Secondly, he is clear that Latin and Greek and other languages should be taught from the outset as instruments not as ends:

'Language is the instrument conveying to us things useful to be known. And if a linguist shall pride himself to have all the tongues that Babel cleft the world into, yet if he have not studied the solid things in them as well as the words and lexicons, he were nothing so much to be esteemed a learned man as any yeoman or tradesman competently wise in the mother dialect only.'

Hence Milton's scorn for too early composition in prose and verse and his reading of Latin and Greek authors for the interest of their content: 'easy and delightful books of education whereof the Greeks have store, as Cebes, Plutarch, and other Socratic discourses. But in Latin we have none'. The truth of that last remark will be clear to anyone who has had to teach Latin and French. How easy to interest a pupil in French, which so soon becomes the vehicle of what is delightful to read! Whereas who can recall one thing in Latin which he read early that gave him then the slightest pleasure? Even Virgil compared with Homer was a bore, a prig, his story full of sacrifices. We cannot now of course go to Latin and Greek to study science, technical and theoretic. But it is a loss that we cannot, a loss that has weakened the claims of a classical education.

The *Areopagitica* again is not a practical treatise on that difficult problem, the limits to be set to freedom of speech. It is an impassioned, prophetic vindication of the invincibility of truth if given a fair field and no favour. Free speech is sadly at a discount today. The extreme wings — Catholic, Fascist, Communist — are united in distrust of the human mind left free to think, and to utter what it thinks. To those whose hope for humanity is still centred in reason Milton's tract remains a splendid prophetic hymn.

By Herbert J. C. Grierson

From *Milton and Wordsworth Poets and Prophets* (Cambridge University Press, 1937)

OF EDUCATION

In June 1644 Milton dedicated to Hartlib his treatise *Of Education*. Little need be said of this production, so easily accessible to all. The most remarkable thing about it — and that which has been oftenest remarked upon — is that Milton is setting their task to colleges of Miltons. He puts upon youths much too heavy a burden, because he himself had carried it lightly. We find here again, therefore, a striking example of that tendency of Milton's, made up of pride, of naïveté, and of a sort of monstrous modesty, to take himself as a normal specimen of human beings, to set down as the rule what fits his case.

Besides, in this whole evolution of his thought, from 1641 to 1645, we must needs notice how complete and absolutely dominant is Milton's egotism. He mostly follows the most advanced minds of his time; occasionally he precedes them. But it is always for personal motives, on private occasions, in safeguard of his own rights. He attacks the prelates from love of liberty, no doubt, but most of all from love of his own liberty, for he has been 'church-outed by the prelates'; 'hence may appear the right I have to meddle in these matters', as he puts it. He discovers the necessity of new laws on divorce — when his own marriage goes wrong. He finds out how narrow-minded the Presbyterians are — when they won't allow him to settle his private affairs as he likes; and the necessity of the freedom of the Press — when they want to prevent him from publishing his tracts. And he writes *Of Education* because, owing to entirely fortuitous circumstances, he has been brought to act as preceptor to a few friends' children. All this might be thought petty? But we may as well think, on the contrary, what a powerful personality was here, a personality which, in the exercise of its normal needs, was brought up against everything that was arbitrary in the laws and customs of his time! This man was under no necessity to think in order to discover the abuses of the social order; all he had to do was to live, and he naturally came to stumble against every prejudice and to trip against every error. He was naïvely surprised, and wondered why everyone did not feel as he did. His egotism and his pride were so deep that they acted as hardly conscious natural forces, as though human nature, trammelled, bound, and imprisoned in all other men, had held to its free course in Milton alone.

For the most remarkable thing of all is that, in our eyes, Milton was each time in the right — against bishops, against presbyters, against censors, against royalists. It is true that he did represent human nature; he was essentially 'representative'; he was a specimen of humanity as it ought to be — if only it were up to sample.

By Denis Saurat

From *Milton Man and Thinker* (Dent, 1944)

Time-Chart

MILTON'S LIFE	HISTORICAL EVENTS
1608, December 9. He is born at his father's house in Bread Street, Cheapside, London.	
	1611. George Abbot, who sympathizes with the doctrines of Puritanism, becomes Archbishop of Canterbury.
	The Authorized Version of the Bible is published.
1620. He enters St. Paul's School.	
1625. He goes up to Christ's College, Cambridge.	1625. James I dies, and Charles I succeeds to the throne.
1626. He is rusticated for a term.	
	1628. Charles signs the Petition of Right.
	William Laud becomes Bishop of London.
1629. He takes his B.A. degree.	1629. Charles dissolves Parliament, and eleven years without parliamentary government begin.
On the Morning of Christ's Nativity.	
1631(?). *L'Allegro* and *Il Penseroso.*	
1632. He takes his M.A. degree.	
He goes to live at Horton, and settles there until 1638.	

MILTON'S LIFE	HISTORICAL EVENTS
	1633. Sir Thomas Wentworth goes as Lord Deputy to Ireland.
	Laud becomes Archbishop of Canterbury.
1634. *Comus* performed at Ludlow Castle.	1634. The first writ for ship-money is issued.
1637. *Lycidas.*	1637. A Star Chamber Decree rigorously controls the Press.
	Laud's attempt to impose a new service-book on the Scottish Kirk causes riots in Edinburgh.
1638. He travels abroad.	
1638–9. He visits Paris, Florence, Rome, Naples, Venice and Geneva.	
1639. He returns to England, settles in London and lodges at St. Bride's Churchyard.	1639. The First Bishops' War with Scotland. It is ended by the Treaty of Berwick in the Scots' favour.
1640–2. He lists epic and dramatic themes, and he plans a tragedy on the subject of *Paradise Lost.*	
1640. He begins teaching his two nephews, Edward and John Phillips.	1640. The Short Parliament.
	The Second Bishops' War, which the Scots win, is ended by the Treaty of Ripon.
He moves to Aldersgate Street.	The Long Parliament.
1641. *Epitaphium Damonis.*	1641. The House of Commons votes to impeach Archbishop Laud.
Of Reformation in England, Of Prelatical Episcopacy and other anti-prelatical pamphlets.	Strafford is executed.

MILTON'S LIFE	HISTORICAL EVENTS
	The Root and Branch Bill to abolish episcopacy is passed by the House of Commons.
	Charles agrees to abolish Star Chamber, ship-money, tunnage and poundage.
	John Amos Comenius comes to England.
	Rebellion begins in Ireland.
	The Grand Remonstrance demands the reform of the Church and the protection of civil rights.
1642. *The Reason of Church Government* and *An Apology for Smectymnuus*.	1642. Charles tries to arrest the Five Members.
He marries Mary Powell, of a Royalist family near Oxford. She leaves him after a few weeks and returns to her parents.	Comenius leaves England.
	Charles raises his standard at Nottingham.
He takes more pupils into his household, and his father comes to live with him.	The battle of Edgehill is indecisive and the Earl of Essex retreats towards London.
1643. *The Doctrine and Discipline of Divorce*.	1643. Royalist successes in the north and west.
	Parliament controls the Press by a strict Licensing Order in June.
	The Assembly of Divines meets at Westminster.
	Parliament ratifies the Solemn League and Covenant with the Scots.
1644. Second edition of *The Doctrine and Discipline of Divorce*.	1644. Fairfax, Cromwell and Leslie's Scots crush the

MILTON'S LIFE

Of Education in June.

The Judgement of Martin Bucer Concerning Divorce.

Areopagitica in November.

1645. Two more divorce tracts: *Tetrachordon* and *Colasterion*.

He is reconciled to his wife, who comes to live with him in London.

They move to a larger house, in Barbican.

He publishes his first volume of poems.

1646. His first child, Anne, is born.

The Powell family, from Oxford, takes refuge temporarily in his home.

1647. His father dies.

He moves to a smaller house in High Holborn.

He gives up schoolmastering.

1648. His second child, Mary, is born.

HISTORICAL EVENTS

Royalists at the Battle of Marston Moor.

Charles is successful in Cornwall, where Essex's infantry surrenders at Lostwithiel.

The second battle of Newbury is an incomplete victory for the Parliamentarians.

1645. Laud, condemned by Act of Attainder, is executed.

Fairfax, Cromwell and the New Model Army end Charles's military power at the battle of Naseby.

1646. Charles gives himself up to the Scots.

Oxford capitulates.

1647. The Scots surrender Charles to Parliament.

The army rises against Parliament and seizes Charles. He flees to the Isle of Wight and enters into the Engagement with the Scots.

1648. Cromwell defeats the Scots under the Duke of Hamilton at the battle of Preston, and ends Charles's hopes of winning the war.

Colonel Pride excludes from Parliament those Presbyterian

MILTON'S LIFE	HISTORICAL EVENTS

<table>
<tr><td></td><td>members who oppose severity to the King, and so 'purges' it. Only the Rump remains.</td></tr>
<tr><td>1649. Tenure of Kings and Magistrates in February.

He is appointed Secretary for Foreign Tongues to the Council of State, in March, and he moves to Whitehall.

Eikonoklastes.</td><td>1649. Charles is tried by a newly appointed High Court of Justice.

Charles is executed in January.

Parliament declares the nation to be a Commonwealth.

Cromwell begins suppressing rebellion in Ireland.</td></tr>
<tr><td></td><td>1650. Cromwell crushes the Scots at the battle of Dunbar.</td></tr>
<tr><td>1651. Defensio pro Populo Anglicano.

His third child, John, is born, but dies in infancy.

He supervises Mercurius Politicus, a government newspaper.

He becomes totally blind, and is granted assistance in office.

He moves from Whitehall to Petty France, Westminster.</td><td>1651. Cromwell and Lambert defeat Charles II at the battle of Worcester.

Union with Scotland and Ireland.</td></tr>
<tr><td>1652. His third daughter, Deborah, is born.

His wife, Mary, dies.</td><td>1652. The First Dutch War begins.

Van Tromp wins sea-battles.</td></tr>
<tr><td></td><td>1653. Blake's victories over Van Tromp end the war.

Cromwell expels Parliament.

Barebone 'Parliament' nominated.

Cromwell becomes Lord Protector, by the Instrument of</td></tr>
</table>

MILTON'S LIFE	HISTORICAL EVENTS
	Government composed by a council of his officers.
1654?–1658? He begins composing *Paradise Lost*.	
1654. *Defensio Secunda*.	1654. The first Parliament of the Protectorate meets.
1655. *Defensio pro Se*.	1655. Cromwell dissolves Parliament.
	Local administration by major-generals is established.
1656. He marries Katherine Woodcock.	1656. Cromwell calls the second Protectorate Parliament.
1657. His fourth daughter is born.	1657. Cromwell refuses the crown offered to him by the *Humble Petition and Advice* of Parliament.
1658. His wife Katherine and their infant daughter die.	1658. Cromwell dissolves Parliament.
	Cromwell dies, and his son Richard succeeds him as Protector.
1659. Two tracts against Church establishment: *A Treatise of Civil Power in Ecclesiastical Causes* and *The Likeliest Means to Remove Hirelings out of the Church*.	1659. A new Parliament assembles, but Richard Cromwell dissolves it.
	The Army restores the Rump.
	Richard Cromwell abdicates.
1660. *The Ready and Easy Way to Establish a Free Commonwealth*.	1660. General Monk marches from Scotland to London. He allows excluded members to return to the Long Parliament.
He is dimissed from office, and takes refuge at a friend's house in Bartholomew Close.	Parliament dissolves voluntarily.

MILTON'S LIFE	HISTORICAL EVENTS
He is arrested, but released on payment of fees.	The Convention Parliament is elected and meets. It votes for the restoration of Charles II.
Eikonoklastes and *Defensio pro Populo Anglicano* are burnt by the hangman.	Charles issues the Declaration of Breda, and returns to London.
He lodges in Holborn, and then moves to Jewin Street.	The Act of Indemnity and Oblivion.
1661? *De Doctrina Christiana* is finished, but it remains unpublished until 1825.	
1663?–1665? He completes *Paradise Lost*.	
1663. He marries Elizabeth Minshull, and they move to a house in Artillery Walk, Bunhill Fields.	
	1664. The Second Dutch War begins.
1665. He and his family move to Chalfont St. Giles, Buckinghamshire, for a short time during the plague.	1665. Plague in London.
	1666. The Great Fire of London.
1667. *Paradise Lost* is published.	1667. The Dutch are in the Medway.
	The Treaty of Breda ends the Dutch War.
1669. His daughters leave home.	
Accedence Commencde Grammar, his Latin grammar in English, is published.	
The History of Britain is published.	

MILTON'S LIFE	HISTORICAL EVENTS
	1670. Charles and Louis XIV sign the Treaty of Dover.
1671. *Paradise Regained* and *Samson Agonistes* are published in one volume.	
1672. *Artis Logicae Plenior Institutio*, his Latin treatise on logic, is published.	1672. The Third Dutch War begins.
	Charles issues a Declaration of Indulgence to Roman Catholics.
1673. *Of True Religion, Heresy, Toleration and the Growth of Popery*.	1673. Parliament opposes the Declaration of Indulgence, and passes the Test Act.
His early poems are republished in an enlarged, second edition.	
His private letters and academic prolusions are published.	
1674. The second edition of *Paradise Lost* is published.	1674. The Third Dutch War ends.
He dies on November 8, and is buried in St. Giles', Cripplegate.	
He leaves three daughters and his widow who dies in 1727.	
Deborah Milton's daughter, Elizabeth Foster, who is the last of his known descendants, dies in 1754.	

Books for Further Reading

Milton's Prose Writings, with an introduction by K. M. Burton ('Everyman's Library', Dent, 1958).

This is a handy, attractive edition. The general introduction and introductions to the selected works are short and helpful.

A Milton Handbook, by James Holly Hanford (Appleton-Century-Crofts, New York, 4th edition, 1954).

A vast collection of material about Milton, his poetry and his prose is presented in a scholarly, clear and brief form. The bibliography is very full.

The Seventeenth Century Background, by Basil Willey (Chatto and Windus, 1934).

These brilliant 'studies in the thought of the age in relation to poetry and religion' include analysis and discussion of Milton's ideas.

Freedom of Expression, a Symposium, edited by Hermon Ould (Hutchinson, 1945).

The impact of *Areopagitica* on a wide variety of twentieth-century writers is shown by these papers. They are based on the conference called by the English Centre of the International P.E.N. in 1944, the tercentenary of *Areopagitica*.

Wife to Mr. Milton, by Robert Graves (Cassell, 1943).

This historical novel tells the story of Milton's first wife. The background is vivid, and Milton's character provocatively unsympathetic.

PRINTED IN GREAT BRITAIN BY ROBERT MACLEHOSE AND CO. LTD
THE UNIVERSITY PRESS, GLASGOW